Number 111
Fall 2006

New Directions for Evaluation

Jean A. King
Editor-in-Chief

Independent Evaluation Consulting

Gail V. Barrington
Dawn Hanson Smart
Editors

INDEPENDENT EVALUATION CONSULTING
Gail V. Barrington, Dawn Hanson Smart (eds.)
New Directions for Evaluation, no. 111
Jean A. King, Editor-in-Chief

Gift 8/07

Microfilm copies of issues and articles are available in 16mm and 35mm, as well as microfiche in 105mm, through University Microfilms Inc., 300 North Zeeb Road, Ann Arbor, Michigan 48106-1346.

New Directions for Evaluation is indexed in Cambridge Scientific Abstracts, Contents Pages in Education, Educational Research Abstracts Online, Higher Education Abstracts, Social Services Abstracts, Sociological Abstracts, and Worldwide Political Sciences Abstracts.

NEW DIRECTIONS FOR EVALUATION (ISSN 1097-6736, electronic ISSN 1534-875X) is part of The Jossey-Bass Education Series and is published quarterly by Wiley Subscription Services, Inc., A Wiley Company, at Jossey-Bass, 989 Market Street, San Francisco, California 94103-1741.

SUBSCRIPTIONS cost $80 for U.S./Canada/Mexico; $104 international. For institutions, agencies, and libraries, $199 U.S.; $239 Canada; $273 international. Prices subject to change.

EDITORIAL CORRESPONDENCE should be addressed to the Editor-in-Chief, Jean A. King, University of Minnesota, 330 Wulling Hall, 86 Pleasant Street SE, Minneapolis, MN 55455.

www.josseybass.com

Editorial Policy and Procedures

New Directions for Evaluation, a quarterly sourcebook, is an official publication of the American Evaluation Association. The journal publishes empirical, methodological, and theoretical works on all aspects of evaluation. A reflective approach to evaluation is an essential strand to be woven through every volume. The editors encourage volumes that have one of three foci: (1) craft volumes that present approaches, methods, or techniques that can be applied in evaluation practice, such as the use of templates, case studies, or survey research; (2) professional issue volumes that present issues of import for the field of evaluation, such as utilization of evaluation or locus of evaluation capacity; (3) societal issue volumes that draw out the implications of intellectual, social, or cultural developments for the field of evaluation, such as the women's movement, communitarianism, or multiculturalism. A wide range of substantive domains is appropriate for *New Directions for Evaluation;* however, the domains must be of interest to a large audience within the field of evaluation. We encourage a diversity of perspectives and experiences within each volume, as well as creative bridges between evaluation and other sectors of our collective lives.

The editors do not consider or publish unsolicited single manuscripts. Each issue of the journal is devoted to a single topic, with contributions solicited, organized, reviewed, and edited by a guest editor. Issues may take any of several forms, such as a series of related chapters, a debate, or a long article followed by brief critical commentaries. In all cases, the proposals must follow a specific format, which can be obtained from the editor-in-chief. These proposals are sent to members of the editorial board and to relevant substantive experts for peer review. The process may result in acceptance, a recommendation to revise and resubmit, or rejection. However, the editors are committed to working constructively with potential guest editors to help them develop acceptable proposals.

Jean A. King, Editor-in-Chief
University of Minnesota
330 Wulling Hall
86 Pleasant Street SE
Minneapolis, MN 55455
e-mail: kingx004@umn.edu

Contents

Editors' Notes

If membership in the American Evaluation Association's Independent Consulting Topical Interest Group (IC TIG) is any indicator, independent consulting in the field of evaluation is growing. We were inspired to work on this volume by the stimulation and insights we have gained over the years from conversations with our peers at AEA's annual conferences—conversations about not just our evaluation projects, but also the business side of consulting and the shared issues and concerns that we face.

We had a vision for this volume. We hoped to:

- Focus on the unique aspects of the independent consultant role in the field of evaluation, exploring the ways in which independent consultants think about, approach, and implement evaluation and how that differs from those of evaluators in other contexts and examining the challenges associated with combining rigorous evaluation skills and good business practice
- Highlight different independent consultant challenges and issues that may span the consultant's life cycle: from novice to intermediate to long-term practitioner
- Explore topics unique to independent consulting such as business start-up and development, personal characteristics and lifestyle issues, marketing, budgeting, project management, communicating with clients, and ethical issues
- Showcase recent IC TIG initiatives, including the results of the recent IC TIG survey as well as the client feedback and peer review processes developed by IC TIG members
- Address emerging issues in the evaluation field that may affect the role of the independent consultant

We chose an open and collaborative process to solicit the chapters for the volume, in part because we wanted to know what would be of interest to other independent consultants—what they wanted to write about and what they wanted to read—and because it is the way we typically work. We invited submissions through EvalTalk and EvalBusiness, the electronic listserv for the IC TIG. We invited authors directly only for the chapters on the IC TIG history and on recent IC TIG professional initiatives. The process paid off as far as we are concerned. The topics covered here represent the day-to-day realities of independent consulting and describe both the fun of our experiences and some of the issues we face.

NEW DIRECTIONS FOR EVALUATION, no. 111, Fall 2006 © Wiley Periodicals, Inc.
Published online in Wiley InterScience (www.interscience.wiley.com) • DOI: 10.1002/ev.190

Our inspiration for the volume grew as we read the manuscripts submitted. We appreciated the authors' thinking and their straightforward writing style, a hallmark, we think, of our work, where efficiency and a down-to-earth manner are essential to maintain business viability. With each chapter, we learned something new or confirmed our own experience, and now we believe other readers will find similar value. Whether you are an independent consultant now, are contemplating a career as a consultant, or are teaching students about the field of evaluation, we think you will find this volume enlightening and timely.

Chapter One provides a brief history of independent consulting within the AEA through the eyes of Deborah G. Bonnet, one of the founders of the IC TIG. Her perspective on the growth and changes she has seen in AEA and the IC TIG give us a sense of how times have changed in the independent evaluation industry.

Chapter Two, by Tania Jarosewich and her coauthors, describes the world of independent consulting in evaluation today, summarizing the results of a 2004 industry survey of the members of the IC TIG. One of our initial dilemmas in putting this volume together was how to describe an independent consultant. This chapter identifies the characteristics of the independent consultants who responded to the survey—their consulting experience, methods, business structures, and incomes. It provides a framework to use when considering the range of options that independent consulting provides.

Three chapters span the life cycle and stages of growth an independent consultant may experience. Chapter Three provides a heartfelt and, for us, familiar look at the questions, concerns, and excitement experienced by someone considering the world of independent consulting in evaluation. Judah J. Viola, currently at DePaul University, shares his hopes and his concerns about this leap into the unknown and highlights many truths about independent consulting that he gained from his conversations with consultants in the field. In Chapter Four, Gail V. Barrington discusses the life cycle of independent evaluation consultants, tracing the stages of growth for a sample of six experienced consultants and looking at the critical incidents that have propelled them from one stage to the next, identifying possible training and support that could be provided at each stage. At the far end of the spectrum, in Chapter Five, Melanie Hwalek and Gregory J. Barber take us through the steps that should be considered toward the end of a consulting career, providing practical information for those who wish to sell their independent consulting businesses or want to do some succession planning.

Four chapters speak directly to the consulting process or to ways of work for independent consultants. In Chapter Six, Morgan Lyons and Maura J. Harrington provide a unique look at the structural and personal learnings they have gleaned over a twenty-year period in their small, entrepreneurial firm. In Chapter Seven, Stephen C. Maack and Jan Upton look at why independent consultants develop collaborations with other evaluators and what some of the benefits and challenges can be. They present their findings looking through the lens of their own collaborative relationship. In Chapter Eight,

Courtney L. Malloy and Patricia A. Yee discuss client relationships and provide a model for effective collaboration with clients.

Two case studies offer a look into specific strategies that independent consultants use. In Chapter Nine, Judith Clegg and Dawn Hanson Smart describe how their firm developed a new line of business and what its benefits have been. In Chapter Ten, Carolyn Cohen presents an interesting evaluation capacity-building strategy on the use of evaluation learning circles and discusses the implications for independent consultants, particularly sole proprietors.

The final two chapters showcase different approaches that independent consultants have developed to obtain feedback from both clients and their peers. For us, this demonstrates the maturity of IC TIG members today and their drive to improve the quality of their work. In Chapter Eleven, Kathleen Dowell, Jean Haley, and Jo Ann Doino-Ingersoll describe the development, testing, and implementation of the client feedback form. In Chapter Twelve, Sally L. Bond and Marilyn L. Ray present a peer review model for independent consultants to critique their peers' evaluation reports. Both of these mechanisms will allow independent consultants to learn and grow professionally in the years ahead.

The chapter authors address the variety of issues independent consultants encounter in their daily work, the kinds of decisions they face, and the joys and challenges they experience. There has never been a compilation like this before. With the burgeoning interest in independent consulting, we believe that this topic is timely and will serve as a springboard to discussion at upcoming conferences and IC TIG meetings.

We include a note of thanks to Jean King for her help in editing this volume. She stepped in and shared some of the workload and provided invaluable assistance and advice as we worked with the authors and completed the final steps in putting together this volume.

Finally, our desire to publish a high-quality volume on independent consulting and the realities of our business was heightened with the loss of our dear coeditor and colleague, Jo Ann Doino-Ingersoll. During the development of this volume, her death was shocking in its suddenness, both saddening us and propelling us into personal reflection about our lives, our work, and our values. We dedicate this volume to her and think that she too would enjoy reading it.

Gail V. Barrington
Dawn Hanson Smart
Editors

GAIL V. BARRINGTON founded Barrington Research Group in 1985 in Calgary, Alberta, Canada, and has been a full-time evaluation consultant ever since.

DAWN HANSON SMART has been senior associate at Clegg & Associates in Seattle, Washington, since 1995 and is a trainer and coach for the Evaluation Forum.

NEW DIRECTIONS FOR EVALUATION • DOI: 10.1002/ev

1

In this retrospective commentary, the author traces the history of AEA's Independent Consulting Topical Interest Group and uses her own consulting practice as a case of how independent evaluation consulting has evolved since 1982.

Independent Consulting and the American Evaluation Association: Twenty Years Later

Deborah G. Bonnet

"I have no use for a fax machine, none at all. Most of my clients are local, we have overnight mail delivery in town, and FedEx is there when I need it. Besides, what's the hurry, anyway?"

I actually remember those words coming out of my mouth at the annual conference of the American Evaluation Association in 1990 in Washington, D.C., where the Independent Consulting Topical Interest Group (IC TIG) was holding its annual business meeting. Marilyn Ray, Burt Perrin, and no doubt other AEA independent consultant pioneers, were correctly aghast, but I was not the only faxless one in the room or the only one who had come around by the time we met again a year later, in Chicago. Help (and prodding) around such nitty-gritty issues of the business of evaluation was an impetus for the IC TIG's formation, and it remains important today.

The TIG goes back a joint meeting held in San Francisco in 1984 of the Evaluation Network (ENet) and the Evaluation Research Society (ERS), two years before the organizations merged to become the AEA. On the fringes of conversations about evaluation theory, paradigms, and methodology, three independent consultants were searching for a more mundane kind of sharing: sources for affordable office supplies, essential clauses for evaluation contracts, and, most of all, a respite from the lonely business of solo evaluation practice. Among the four hundred or so (mostly university and

NEW DIRECTIONS FOR EVALUATION, no. 111, Fall 2006 © Wiley Periodicals, Inc.
Published online in Wiley InterScience (www.interscience.wiley.com) • DOI: 10.1002/ev.191

government people) in attendance, Katheryn Hecht, Tara Davis Knott, and I found one another, and the TIG was born.

In 1985 ENet, ERS, and the Canadian Evaluation Society met together in Toronto. The IC TIG sponsored two sessions: "Marketing Evaluation Services" and "Striking Out on Your Own." We followed that pattern for a number of years: one conference session for "ourselves" (that is, relatively advanced or technical) and one for curious and prospective independent consultants. A session at ENet 1981 had been pivotal in my garnering the courage to go independent, and we all felt an obligation to offer our restless salaried colleagues guidance and support in following our paths—or not.

Other than sponsoring sessions at AEA, the TIG was not particularly ambitious in the early years. Tara Knott led a valiant effort to gather up résumés, but it was before fax machines, not to mention e-mail attachments, so even if we had succeeded in constructing a database, there was no easy way of getting it out. There were a couple of newsletters and a few brief articles in the "Consultants' Corner," published in *Evaluation Practice,* the precursor of the *American Journal of Evaluation.*

In 1988 the TIG sponsored four sessions, including one where we exchanged work samples in advance to critique one another's work. In 1989 Steve Mayer surveyed the 226 registered members of the TIG about conference topics that would interest them; 27 people responded. Herein lies a perennial problem: the TIG membership has always been much larger than the number of independent consultants—by how much, we have never known—and active participants in TIG activities are a smaller group still. AEA members are allowed up to five TIG memberships; a side effect of this policy is that people with only casual interest in a topic sign up for TIGs but may not actively participate in TIG activities. Despite this, our conference sessions have been well attended and well received, and, whatever the actual numbers are, we know they have grown by leaps and bounds.

By 1992 the TIG membership stood at 293; in 2004, 713. Today it is 834, 18 percent of AEA's total membership. Attendance at TIG business meetings at the annual conference, a fairly good indicator of the TIG's core, was in the single digits throughout the 1980s. In 1991 it surged to 14, but dropped back down to 10 the following year. In recent years the crowds have spilled into the hallways. The meetings are less cozy, for sure, but better organized, and they continue to nourish the collegial connections that remain at the heart of the TIG.

The IC TIG has grown not just in numbers but also in accomplishments. In 2004 it sponsored thirteen sessions at AEA's annual conference in addition to a business meeting. Topics have become more sophisticated, with a particular emphasis on ethics. In recent years the TIG has embarked on three valuable projects, each reported in this volume: (1) a survey of TIG members' business practices, evaluation services, demographics, and so on; (2) a service whereby clients evaluate evaluators' performance; and (3) an ongoing process for peer review of draft evaluation reports. From 1993 through 2005, Gail Barrington offered a workshop on consulting skills for evaluators who were thinking of starting their own business as a presession to AEA's annual conferences, a service that will be interrupted while she serves as an AEA board member. Independent consultants, including business owners, have been represented on the AEA board since 1994, when I joined; now there are two: Melanie Hwalek as well as Gail.

Chapter Two in this volume is the best and only source of data about independent evaluation consulting, covering demographic characteristics of TIG members, consulting experience, services, methods, business structures, income, and more. Results are compared to a similar study conducted in 1992. Two highlights stand out:

- The business has feminized further but achieved some ethnic diversification. In 1992, 60 percent of the survey respondents were female and 98 percent were white. In 2004, 71 percent were female and 81 percent white.
- We are making more money. The median gross personal business income of full-time, self-employed respondents increased from $60,795 in 1991 to $75,000 in 2003 (adjusted for inflation).

The results aside, differences in how the studies were done speak volumes about how both the TIG and the consulting business changed between 1992 and 2004. I did the 1992 study myself. We talked a little about its scope at the 1991 TIG business meeting, and I had a clear charge to do the survey on the TIG's behalf, but I have no recollection or record of any review of the draft instrument or report other than by the editor of *Evaluation Practice*. It was mailed, of course, with no follow-up. Arguably, by the standards of the day, I should have piloted the survey and mailed reminder notices. But snail mail was all we had, plus a small budget and my own limits on volunteerism, so nobody complained (as far as I know). The 2004 survey, in contrast, was developed through an interactive process involving multiple iterations through collaborative communications among the five authors, then pilot-tested by five other independent consultants prior to being finalized. The survey was made available to AEA and IC TIG members in print and online forms. It was distributed at the 2004 annual conference and put online, with the link e-mailed to all TIG members twice and posted on the IC TIG's electronic list, EvalBusiness. In short, the 2004 survey was more professional, more collaborative, and yet cheaper in out-of-pocket costs made possible by advances in technology, but also reflecting higher expectations and, in my opinion, more stature for independent consulting.

This review of the TIG's evolution concludes with a case: my own. I started in business in 1982 after leaving a firm that had grown to twenty people, fueled largely by generous federal funding for educational research and development that dried up the day Ronald Reagan took office. My entrepreneurial urge had been mounting for several years, and many factors went into the timing of my leap, but what made my dream feasible was the introduction of the personal computer. Without one, operating a professional practice without a secretary (a correct term at the time) was hard to imagine: Who would do your typing? I bought one of the first IBM PCs to roll off the assembly line, thereby solving the problem of document production. It had no hard disk, just a single five-and-a-quarter-inch floppy drive and 64K of RAM, no mouse, but two printers, one dot matrix (for drafts and accounting), and one daisy wheel (which looked like real typing).

I was a late adopter of the laptop computer (1998) and cell phone (2002), both freeing and boundary dissolving in their own ways. I reserved the domain DBonnet.com in 2000, but to my disgrace, still have no Web site, today's equivalent of a business card and a ticket to AEA's consultant referral service (http://eval.org/find_an_evaluator/evaluator_ search.asp). I promise myself: by the time this chapter is published, it *will* be up and running.

DEBORAH G. BONNET *does business as DBonnet Associates in Indianapolis, Indiana.*

NEW DIRECTIONS FOR EVALUATION • DOI: 10.1002/ev

This chapter summarizes the results of the 2004 Independent Consulting Topical Interest Group Industry Survey. Respondents provided information on demographic characteristics, consulting experience, services, methods, business structures, and income.

Independent Consulting Topical Interest Group: 2004 Industry Survey

Tania Jarosewich, Victoria L. Essenmacher, Christina Olenik Lynch, Jennifer E. Williams, Jo Ann Doino-Ingersoll

The American Evaluation Association's (AEA) Independent Consulting Topical Interest Group (IC TIG) has a membership of over eight hundred individuals who generally work as sole proprietors, in partnerships, or in small consulting firms. Well over a decade ago, the IC TIG conducted a survey of its membership (Bonnet, 1992). To gather current data with which to better understand its membership, the IC TIG disseminated a similar survey in the fall of 2004. Results, provided here in a format similar to Bonnet's industry survey article, include the background, services, clients, and business structures and operations of ICs, as well as a section on independent consultants' perceptions of business. This chapter compares Bonnet's findings with the results of the 2004 industry survey, identifies study limitations, and discusses trends for the future.

Methods

The goal of the 2004 IC TIG Survey was to learn about business operations, types of clients and work, business success indicators, marketing, evaluation methods, and demographics. The survey was developed through a collaborative process among the authors that began with a review of the 1992 survey items (Bonnet, 1992) and analysis of additional topics thought to be important. The final survey contained thirty-three items, some overlapping

NEW DIRECTIONS FOR EVALUATION, no. 111, Fall 2006 © Wiley Periodicals, Inc.
Published online in Wiley InterScience (www.interscience.wiley.com) • DOI: 10.1002/ev.192

with the previous survey and several of them new. The survey had nineteen items for all respondents and an additional fourteen for respondents who were self-employed consultants *and* who had operated their business for a full year during 2003. The instrument was pilot-tested with five independent consultants prior to being finalized, and pilot group results were incorporated into the final version of the survey.

AEA and IC TIG members could complete either a print version during the 2004 annual AEA conference or an online version of the survey. Potential respondents were informed of the survey at the annual AEA conference, via TIG-wide e-mail, and through the TIG electronic discussion list. A list of IC TIG members' e-mail addresses was obtained from AEA. All IC TIG members with a valid e-mail address received an e-mail that included an invitation to participate in the project and a link to the online version of the survey. TIG members subsequently received three reminder e-mails. The link to the survey was also posted on the IC TIG's electronic list, EvalBusiness, with a reminder of the closing date of the survey.

Of the 713 IC TIG members in 2004, 261 (37 percent) independent consultants completed the survey: 242 the online version and 19 the paper version. This return rate represents a substantial improvement over the 1992 survey, which was completed by 20 percent of the TIG members surveyed (58 of 293 members).

Results

Responses were imported into SPSS and analyzed to provide descriptive statistics, analysis of differences in proportions, t-tests, and regression analysis. The responses from the open-ended items were coded into categories and the categories summarized.

Background. Seventy-one percent of the 261 survey participants were female and 29 percent male. Forty-nine percent ($N = 127$) were full time, self-employed; 43 percent part time, self-employed ($N = 111$); 8 percent ($N = 21$) employees of independent consulting firms; and 1 percent ($N = 2$) identified themselves as "other." Forty-eight respondents (18 percent) were faculty members. Those who were self-employed consultants and operated their business for a full year during 2003 ($N = 152$) reported that they had operated their consulting business an average of 8.2 years, with a range from 1 year to 27 years. Self-employed consultants who had prior consulting experience ($N = 93$) reported a mean of 8.0 years consulting experience prior to starting their business, ranging from 6 months to 25 years. Thirty-seven percent (37 percent) had no prior experience.

The majority of respondents were white (81 percent) and female (71 percent). The next largest racial groups represented were black (7 percent) and Hispanic/Latino (5 percent). The ages of the respondents ranged from under thirty to seventy or older, with the majority aged forty to fifty-nine years old (64 percent). About 68 percent of the 261 respondents indicated

NEW DIRECTIONS FOR EVALUATION • DOI: 10.1002/ev

Figure 2.1. Respondents' Race/Ethnicity

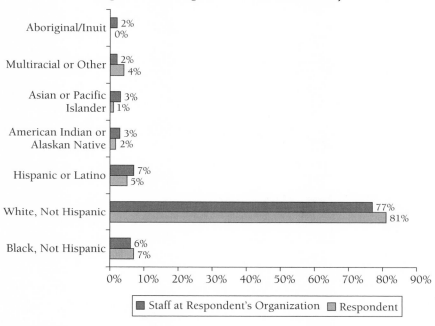

Note: N = 243.

that they have, including themselves, at least one female employee, and 37 percent reported having at least one male staff. As indicated in Figure 2.1, the racial breakdown for employees was similar, with 77 percent white, 7 percent Hispanic/Latino, and 6 percent black.

Of the 237 respondents who reported their highest attained levels of education, 55 percent earned a doctoral degree, 41 percent a master's degree, 4 percent a bachelor's degree, and less than 1 percent some college. Respondents majored in a variety of subjects, including education (28 percent), psychology (22 percent), evaluation (18 percent), sociology (8 percent), statistics (5 percent), anthropology (3 percent), and economics (3 percent). Of the 41 percent who selected "Other," only two majors were identified by more than 2 percent of respondents: public health (5 percent) and public administration (5 percent).

Approximately one-quarter of the respondents (24 percent) were located in the midwestern United States and another 22 percent in the South Atlantic United States. A smaller proportion had their primary office location in the northeastern United States (17 percent), the Pacific states (15 percent), outside the United States (8 percent), the Mountain states (7 percent), and other southern states (7 percent).

NEW DIRECTIONS FOR EVALUATION • DOI: 10.1002/ev

Figure 2.2. Most Common Areas in Which Services Are Provided

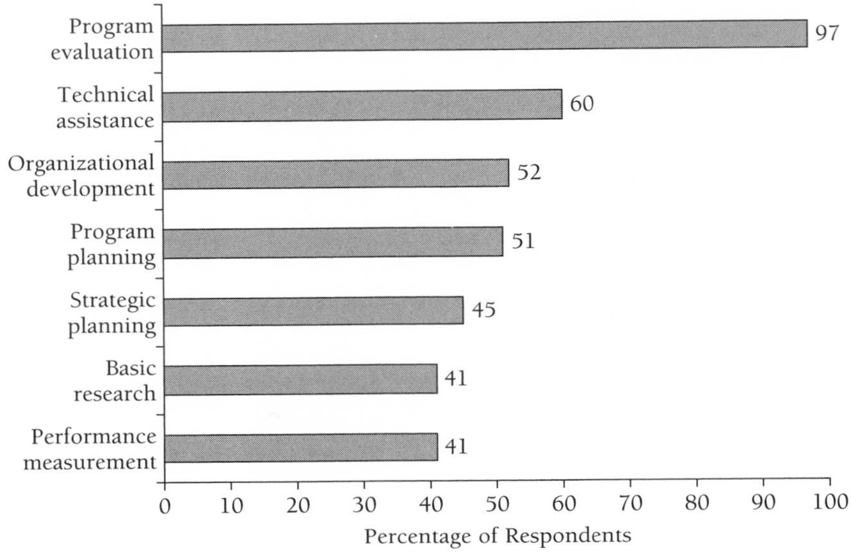

Note: N = 243.

Services. As indicated in Figure 2.2, 97 percent of respondents provide program evaluation, 60 percent provide technical assistance, 52 percent offer organizational development, and 51 percent program planning services. Other areas were listed less frequently.

Table 2.1 identifies the top fourteen services consultants provide to clients. The seven most frequently identified services were survey/questionnaire development (92 percent), report writing (91 percent), qualitative analysis (87 percent), development of data collection tools (84 percent), focus groups (81 percent), evaluation frameworks/logic models (78 percent), and statistical analysis (77 percent). A large majority, 90 percent of respondents, indicated that they provide a mix of qualitative and quantitative services, with only 5 percent each saying they offer mostly quantitative or qualitative services.

Respondents reported whether employees (including themselves) or subcontractors conduct a series of evaluation activities. Employees most frequently complete report writing, in-person interviews, literature review, field observations, focus groups, statistical analysis, telephone interviews, data entry, and mass mailing. Accounting/taxes and transcription were most often completed by subcontractors.

Clients. Independent consultants conduct business in a wide variety of settings. As indicated in Table 2.2, the majority of respondents reported providing evaluation services for nonprofit organizations (73 percent),

Table 2.1. Types of Services Provided to Clients

	Number	Percentage
Survey/questionnaire development	221	92
Report writing	220	91
Qualitative analysis	210	87
Development of data collection tools	203	84
Focus groups	196	81
Evaluation frameworks/logic models	188	78
Statistical analysis	186	77
Design/delivery of training/professional development	139	58
Measurement	130	54
Data processing	115	48
Evaluability assessments	70	29
Writing entire grant proposals	67	28
Information system design	58	24
Test develop/validation/standardization	50	21

Note: Total number of respondents = 241.

Table 2.2. Industries in Which Independent Consultants Provide Evaluation Services

Settings	Number	Percentage
Nonprofit organizations	176	73.0
Community-based organizations	172	71.4
Social service (for example, substance abuse, teen pregnancy, juvenile justice)	146	60.6
Local/state/federal government	134	55.6
K-12 education	133	55.2
Health care	98	40.7
Foundations	85	35.3
Postsecondary education	71	29.5
Private sector/corporate	68	28.2
Technical/vocational education	37	15.4
International	37	15.4
Other	25	10.4
Environmental programs	21	8.7

Note: Total number of respondents = 241.

community-based organizations (71 percent), social service settings (61 percent), local/ state/federal government (56 percent), and K-12 education (55 percent). Approximately one-quarter (24 percent) conducted business within their own state, province, or region, while almost one-third of respondents (32 percent) described a national clientele. Smaller percentages of independent consultants worked with organizations that were multistate/province/regional (16 percent), local (15 percent), or international (13 percent).

NEW DIRECTIONS FOR EVALUATION • DOI: 10.1002/ev

Business Structures and Operations. The majority of the respondents (71 percent) conduct their consulting work in their homes, with less than a quarter (22 percent) having a separate office outside the home. Seven percent work in other places. Legal forms of business under which independent consultants are formed include sole proprietorships (50 percent), for-profit corporations (35 percent), nonprofit corporations (4 percent), and partnerships (3 percent). Seven percent identified themselves as "Other." Responses that fell within this category included those in the process of setting up their business structure ($n = 8$), having no business structure ($n = 5$), and functioning as "doing business as" ($n = 2$).

Survey respondents said they spent a majority of their time (63 percent) conducting evaluations and providing client services. They spent approximately equal amounts of time managing their business operations (15 percent) as generating new business (14 percent). Less than 10 percent of their time was spent receiving professional development.

Self-employed consultants who operated their business for a full year in 2003 were asked to rate and rank the most and least effective methods of marketing. The most efficient methods of marketing were referrals/word of mouth and recurring business, followed by guest speaking, presentations at conferences, pro bono work, scholarly writing/publishing, responding to requests for proposals (RFP), and community service/volunteer work. One hundred thirty-seven respondents identified which method was most effective. The most frequent response was referral/word of mouth ($n = 81$), followed by recurring business ($n = 41$) and responding to RFPs ($n = 8$). Least effective methods of generating new business, identified by 111 respondents, included responding to RFPs ($n = 18$) and Web site ($n = 15$). Clearly, independent consultants have different success rates and perceptions of the effectiveness of responding to RFPs for procuring new business opportunities.

Table 2.3 summarizes results from the business operations data asked only of consultants who were self-employed *and* who operated their business for a full year during 2003: gross business revenue, personal gross income, and hours worked. The table includes available data from the 1992 survey, which reported business operations figures for 1991 in 1991 dollars, and the current survey, which reported data from 2003. (Reported numbers have not been adjusted for inflation and are taken directly from each survey.) Overall, 2003 business revenues ranged from $27,000 to $2 million, with a median of $120,000. The median 2003 personal income for full-time self-employed independent consultants was $75,000 and ranged from $12,000 to $350,000. Full-time independent consultants with employees ($n = 34$) had a median personal gross income of $82,070 a year, 28 percent higher than solo practitioners ($64,000, $n = 28$). The differences in personal incomes were not significant, $t(60) = -0.87$, $p = 0.39$. Further exploration revealed that income and number of employees did not show a clear linear relationship with this sample of independent consultants. This relationship is discussed later in the chapter.

NEW DIRECTIONS FOR EVALUATION • DOI: 10.1002/ev

Table 2.3. 1991 and 2003 Independent Consultant Business Performance

| | | 1991 | | | | 2003 | | |
	N	Low	Fiftieth Percentile	High	N	Low	Fiftieth Percentile	High
Full-time self-employed								
Gross business revenues	26	$17,500	$83,301	$2,000,000	77	$27,000	$120,000	$2,000,000
Personal business income	26	$15,000	$45,000	$100,000	68	$12,000	$75,000	$350,000
Hours worked	NA	NA	NA	NA	62	200	1,910	3,952
Part-time self-employed								
Hours worked	NA	NA	NA	NA	24	63	950	2,500

In 2003, full-time consultants worked a total number of hours between 200 (less than 4 hours a week) to 3,592 (just under a 70-hour workweek for 52 weeks). The median total hours worked was 1,910 (equivalent to 40-hour work weeks with four weeks of vacation, holidays, and personal days). Twenty-five percent of full-time, self-employed consultants worked 1,440 hours, fewer than 30 hours per work week, assuming four weeks of vacation, holidays, and personal days. Another 25 percent worked between 30 and 40 hours per week on average.

Full-time self-employed consultants' hourly rate results, illustrated in Table 2.4, ranged from $40 to $219 an hour, with a median of $100 per hour. The reported hourly rate for Ph.D.s (average of $114 per hour) is significantly higher than that of master's-level consultants ($93 per hour), $t(78) = 2.46$, $p = 0.02$. Full-time self-employed evaluators billed at a significantly higher hourly rate than part-time independent consultants: an average of $105 and $88 per hour, respectively, $t(122) = 2.22$, $p = 0.03$. Differences in rates between geographical regions for full-time self-employed consultants are also shown in Table 2.4. Significance analyses by region and education level could not be conducted because too few consultants were represented in the different regions.

Table 2.5 shows the results from a regression analysis examining predictors of self-employed consultants' personal incomes. Predictor variables entered into the regression were total numbers of hours worked in 2003; total number of estimated billable hours worked in 2003; hourly billing rate; gross business revenue for 2003; number of years in business as a consultant; number of years of prior experience in evaluation prior to becoming self-employed; total number of employees, including oneself; and level of education. Due to a lack of clear linear relationships in several cases and a relatively small number of cases that contained all variables ($n = 68$), results in this analysis should be interpreted with caution.

As Table 2.5 shows, the three significant predictors of personal income are gross business revenue, number of billable hours worked, and number of employees. Results show that in general, evaluators with the largest personal incomes tend also to have larger business revenue, more billable hours worked, and fewer employees. The total number of hours worked is not significantly related to personal income, and hourly rate, years in business, years of prior experience, and level of education do not significantly predict the amount of personal income an evaluator derives from self-employment.

Independent Consultants' Perceptions About the Business. Ninety-three full-time and 47 part-time consultants answered questions about their perceptions of the success of their business. Twenty-nine percent of full-time and 13 percent of part-time self-employed consultants agreed they were making "well above an adequate living," and 31 percent of full-time and 19 percent of part-time self-employed consultants agreed that they were making "just above an adequate living." Another 35 percent of full-time and 38 percent of part-time consultants were

Table 2.4. Independent Consultant Hourly Fees, 2003

	Minimum	Twenty-Fifth Percentile	Fiftieth Percentile	Seventy-Fifth Percentile	Maximum	Mean	N
Full-time self-employed							
All self-employed full time	$40	$80	$100	$125	$219	$105	85
Education							
Ph.D.	$50	$84	$100	$135	$219	$114	42
Master's	$40	$71	$100	$100	$160	$93	38
Primary office location							
U.S. Midwest	$40	$80	$100	$125	$200	$104	24
U.S. Mountain states	$50	$56	$75	$125	$188	$93	7
U.S. Northeast	$67	$85	$125	$150	$175	$122	8
U.S. Pacific states	$63	$83	$100	$110	$219	$104	13
U.S. South Atlantic states	$48	$80	$100	$120	$200	$106	19
Other U.S. southern states	$60	$60	$75	$114	$187	$91	6
Outside the United States	$64	$83	$99	$119	$190	$106	8
Part-time self-employed							
All self-employed part time	$35	$55	$75	$125	$175	$88	39
Education							
Ph.D.	$40	$59	$75	$125	$175	$90	23
Master's	$35	$50	$75	$100	$150	$81	15

Note: The number of self-employed part-time consultants was too small to analyze by primary office location.

Table 2.5. Regression Predicting Evaluator's Personal Income

	Beta	T	p	Zero-Order	Partial
Hours worked	−0.03	−0.19	0.85	0.60	−0.03
Hours billed	0.34	2.64	0.01*	0.58	0.33
Hourly rate	0.07	0.95	0.35	0.24	0.12
Gross business revenue	1.10	9.83	0.00*	0.74	0.79
Years of business	−0.00	−0.04	0.97	0.11	0.00
Years of prior experience	−0.01	−0.174	0.86	0.11	−0.02
Number of employees including self	−0.58	−5.024	0.00*	0.39	−0.55
Level of education	−0.08	−1.274	0.21	−0.18	−0.17

Note: R^2 = 0.81. Adjusted R^2 = 0.78.
*p < .01.

making "an adequate living, but not more than adequate," and the last 4 percent of full-time and 30 percent of part-time consultants reported they "did not make an adequate living."

Of the 132 consultants who described 378 advantages of being an independent consultant, the three top advantages were flexibility of schedule and time (26 percent), the autonomy of being their own boss (18 percent), and the ability to choose projects and clients (15 percent). The next largest category of responses accounted for only 6 percent of respondents. Although flexibility and autonomy may be related, responses coded within the "autonomy" category had broad words such as *autonomy, freedom,* and *independence.* Responses coded as "flexibility of schedule and time" were more specific comments about what independent consultants most liked.

The top disadvantages of being an independent consultant were not as clear. The highest response category was reported by 15 percent of independent consultants, and the following seven categories of responses were within 10 percent of the highest. Of 340 responses from 130 consultants, the top eight disadvantages listed were "it all depends on you"/have to do it all (15 percent), inconsistent/unpredictable income (11 percent), professional isolation (10 percent), general instability/uncertainty (8 percent), having to get new work/market/sell/network (7 percent), the long hours/no separate personal life (7 percent), inconsistent/unpredictable workload (6 percent), and cost and/or lack of fringe benefits (5 percent).

Comparisons of the 1992 and 2004 TIG Industry Survey. Although the sample size in Bonnet's (1992) survey (N = 58) and the current survey (N = 261) were different, some comparisons can be made between the findings of the two surveys. First, it appears that independent consultants are now serving more diverse clients. Bonnet reported that respondents worked most often with nonprofit organizations, state government, other consulting groups as subcontractors, private business, federal government, schools, foundations, local government, and universities. In the current survey, respondents reported working with these types of organizations as well as community-based organizations, health care institutions, social services, international groups, and environmental programs.

Second, there are differences in the legal forms of business under which independent consultants are currently formed. Although the most frequently identified form of business reported by Bonnet (1992) and in the current survey was sole proprietor, this proportion has significantly decreased from 73 percent in 1992 to 50 percent in 2004 ($z = 3.33$, $p = .00$). Similarly, there are significantly fewer nonprofit corporations, $z = 4.01$, $p = .00$ (6 percent 1992; 4 percent 2004) and partnerships, $z = 2.11$, $p = .035$, (8 percent 1992; 3 percent 2004) in 2004 than in 1992. The proportion of for-profit corporations has significantly increased, $z = 3.01$, $p = .00$, with 35 percent of independent consultants currently organized as LLC, S Corporations, or C Corporations (types of business structures identified in U.S. tax law) as compared with 14 percent reporting these types of business entities in 1992.

Finally, as illustrated in Table 2.3, the reported median gross business revenues were $83,301 in 1991 and $120,000 in 2003. Adjusting for inflation (http://data.bls.gov/cgi-bin/cpicalc.pl), the 1991 median amount translates into $112,540. So it appears that median gross business revenues have increased in the past twelve years. The reported median personal gross income increased at a greater rate when taking inflation into account, from $45,000 in 1991 ($60,795 in 2003 dollars) to $75,000 in 2003.

Discussion

The 2004 IC TIG Survey respondents were primarily white, female respondents, with employees of similar types of ethnic and gender diversity, fairly representative of the TIG's membership as a whole. The majority had terminal degrees in the social sciences. The respondents, mostly aged forty to fifty-nine, could be considered seasoned consulting professionals, with self-employed independent consultants who owned their business in 2003, having about eight years of consulting experience prior to starting their business. Geographically, respondents were scattered across the United States, with almost half in the Midwest and South Atlantic states. The majority of survey respondents conducted their business out of their homes, and many served clients nationwide. Their legal forms of business primarily fell into sole proprietorship or for-profit corporation. The most effective marketing strategies identified were referrals/word of mouth and recurring business.

Over half of the respondents indicated that at least 80 percent of their business consists of evaluation services. The most frequently provided services were survey/questionnaire development, report writing, data analysis, development of data collection tools, development of logic frameworks, and focus groups. They also reported conducting their business with a wide variety of clients, such as nonprofit organizations, community-based organizations, governmental organizations, and educational institutions.

In terms of business indicators of success, full-time self-employed consultants appeared to be doing quite well. The 2003 median personal income for this group was $75,000. Half of the group reported that they were making "just above" or "well above" an adequate living. The results of the analysis suggested that consultants maximized personal income from self-employment by limiting the number of nonbillable hours worked. One category of evaluators who drew the largest personal income from their business was solo consultants who worked from home and had low overhead expenses. The evaluator working from home using only subcontractors may be able to absorb a greater percentage of the billing rate as personal income. The evaluator with several employees is probably working fewer billable hours while simultaneously using some of the billing rate to pay for such things as office rent, communications systems, and nonbillable employee salaries (for example, a bookkeeper). Having a larger number of employees provides the potential for more personal income if it is planned carefully so that billing rates cover the overhead expenditures.

The primary perceived advantages of being an independent consultant were flexibility of schedule and time, autonomy of being one's own boss, and ability to choose projects and clients. Primary disadvantages included having to "do it all," unpredictable income, and professional isolation.

Limitations of the Survey. A potential limitation of the 2004 IC TIG Survey is the possibility of a nonrepresentative sample of respondents, as only 261 of 713 TIG members completed a survey. However, it is unclear what percentage of IC TIG members work as consultants and what percentage are interested in moving into consulting or are simply curious about the work of the TIG for other reasons.

Trends for the Future. The increase in the number of IC TIG members from 293 in Bonnet's 1992 survey to 834 in 2006 suggests that the business of independent evaluation consulting is growing. With this increase in membership comes the additional variation in business formation and a higher percentage of for-profit as opposed to nonprofit evaluation firms. Independent consultants also seem to be working with a greater variety of organizations, such as community-based efforts, health care institutions, and environmental programs, in addition to educational institutions, government, nonprofits, and foundations among others. Most important, the rewards for working as an independent consultant are becoming more enticing, with hourly rates and personal incomes approaching those of other popular professions.

NEW DIRECTIONS FOR EVALUATION • DOI: 10.1002/ev

Reference

Bonnet, D. "Independent Evaluation Consulting TIG: 1992 Industry Survey." *Evaluation Practice,* 1992, *13*(3), 225–231.

TANIA JAROSEWICH is president of Censeo Group, an evaluation consulting firm in Cleveland, Ohio.

VICTORIA L. ESSENMACHER is a partner of SPEC Associates, a research and evaluation firm in Detroit, Michigan.

CHRISTINA OLENIK LYNCH is a partner in the consulting firm Partners in Evaluation and Planning in Sykesville, Maryland.

JENNIFER E. WILLIAMS is president of the consulting firm J. E. Williams and Associates in Cincinnati, Ohio.

JO ANN DOINO-INGERSOLL (1956–2006) was president of Strategic Research, an education and human services consulting firm in Mahwah, New Jersey.

3

The author reflects on his hopes and fears as he considers an independent consulting career.

I Want to Be an Independent Consultant: Considerations Before Taking the Plunge

Judah J. Viola

During my second year of graduate school, a few friends approached me with the idea of taking on independent consulting projects together or perhaps even starting an evaluation consulting company. I was thrilled and anxious all at once. But more than anything else, I had lots of questions that needed answers before fully committing myself to a business: What would it be like to work independent of an established firm or institution such as the university, where I was comfortable conducting research and evaluations? Would a consulting path provide me with sufficient income? Would I find the work fulfilling? What qualities are required to succeed as an independent evaluation consultant?

I began to search for answers by reading start-up guides and recommended books on the consulting field (for example, Bellman, 1990; Block, 1999; Edwards and Edwards, 1996; Lukas, 1998). I started to identify the ways that being a sole proprietor was distinct from working for a consulting firm. As a sole proprietor, I would have to find my own clients and would not benefit from the structural supports provided by an established company and experienced staff. There would be no existing infrastructure, human resources (for example, colleagues, supervisors), health benefits, professional counsel (legal, accounting)—not even a steady paycheck. Moreover, I realized that it would not be enough to simply survive as an independent consultant. It was critical for me to take on new contracts from

NEW DIRECTIONS FOR EVALUATION, no. 111, Fall 2006 © Wiley Periodicals, Inc.
Published online in Wiley InterScience (www.interscience.wiley.com) • DOI: 10.1002/ev.193

23

clients whose work fit with my own values. I also hoped those projects would be of interest to me and that I could make selections based on my workload.

My reading uncovered important considerations, but I knew that learning directly from experienced evaluation consultants could provide further insight into what it would actually be like to start and build an independent consulting practice. Therefore, I decided to pick the brains of current experts in the field. I surveyed thirty evaluators and interviewed fifteen with extensive experience consulting for nonprofit and government organizations through a variety of business entities (for example, part-time and full-time sole proprietors, small business owners, nonprofits, and employees for small and medium-sized evaluation consulting firms). I asked these expert participants to describe their start-up experiences, trace the general progression of their careers, and provide recommendations for those of us beginning our careers. The experts' responses piqued my interest, heightened my fears, and largely fueled my desire to become an independent consultant.

Driven by Hope

Perhaps the foremost reason I became interested in consulting was my realization over time that focusing solely on theoretical or academic work would not completely fulfill my drive to have a tangible impact on people's lives. I wanted, and still want, to make a contribution by working with real people toward solving real problems at individual and organizational levels. Seeing the people within an organization improve their programming as the result of our collaboration would feel like immediate gratification compared to the pace and potential outcomes of the academic research and publication process.

The most gratifying aspect of talking with practicing consultants was hearing how satisfied they were with their work. Their enthusiasm for their autonomous initiatives and collaborations was palpable, even over the telephone. Again and again I heard how rewarding it was to have their values and work in full alignment. When I combined the enjoyment of their work with their generosity in sharing their time and their engagement in telling their stories, it was not difficult to understand why I wanted to break into the profession.

Another draw to independent evaluation consulting was the opportunity to apply my skills to a wide variety of topical areas while continuing to grow and learn throughout my career. In talking with practicing independent consultants, I was pleased to learn that the scope of their projects was as varied as their personalities. I heard from consultants who partnered with organizations in education, theater, agriculture, affordable housing, job training, disability services, immigrant advocacy, domestic violence, public health, and more.

The work of a consultant, it became clear, was dynamic, challenging, and energizing. While both traditional process and outcome evaluations were mentioned as the bulk of the work completed, many consultants also assisted organizations in empowerment evaluations and building internal evaluation capacity. Some independent consultants provided trainings or helped build structures for data collection and record keeping, whereas others aided their clients in writing evaluation activities into their grant proposals, walked clients through strategic planning, or guided them in logic modeling processes. I am now confident that the variety in potential clients and activities will continue to keep the word *bored* out of my vocabulary.

Slowed by Fears and Anxieties

While it was encouraging to hear about the variety of activities I could take part in and the great potential for job satisfaction, many of my preexisting concerns were also validated. Having recently completed my doctorate, I worry now that as an independent consultant, particularly in a sole proprietorship, I may not be able to support a family while simultaneously paying off student loans. Consulting involves continually contracting to do new, time-limited jobs. As a result, the work may not always be consistent enough to provide a steady income. Experienced consultants informed me that during their first few years in business, they were inundated with more projects than they could complete, and at other times there were droughts (for example, during a recession with lots of budget cuts or at periods within the funding cycle when nonprofits slowed their spending). I was repeatedly warned that at the start, I should not expect to gain the preponderance of my income through consulting.

Financial strains were not my only concern. What were the time demands of an independent consulting practice? I am motivated and prepared to work hard, but I also hope that the transition out of graduate school will be into a lower-stress environment with more substantive time for family and friends. These hopes were dashed when most of the consultants I interviewed spoke of long workdays and little time for personal life, at least for the first years. Most consultants explained that achieving a healthy balance between professional and personal life would remain a challenge for some years. It was especially disconcerting for me to hear consistently of difficulties concerning time management, because somewhere in my desires for a consulting life, I looked forward to avoiding the publish-or-perish environment of academia, which I felt would reduce the likelihood of work demands interfering with personal time.

In the face of the long hours and limited personal time I now have in the academic arena, having a network of colleagues readily available has been crucial. I have come to rely on professors and students for support and guidance in my graduate career and often get my best ideas through dialogue with colleagues. Would becoming an independent consultant mean losing this network? Would my work or my emotional well-being suffer as a result? Independent consultants, including the sole proprietors I spoke with, reported that they combat loneliness by getting involved in professional organizations and teaming up with other consultants on larger jobs. They also took advantage of slower periods in the work cycle to connect more fully with family, friends, and past clients. Despite such tactics, I continue to wonder whether talking with other evaluators or researchers by e-mail or the occasional social gathering will provide enough professional support.

As I continue to learn more about the process of getting started as an independent evaluation consultant, I realize that in addition to my initial concerns and the initial excitement associated with keeping my career goals, personal values, and emotional insecurities in line, there are many nuts-and-bolts issues yet left to explore. I still need some extended self-examination to articulate clearly what useful services I can provide organizations. Having only recently learned the difference between a limited liability corporation and a partnership and how to file estimated taxes, I continue to realize how much there is to know about running a small business. Of the experts I spoke with, those who used accountants from the start were happy they did, and those who did not regretted the decision. Nonetheless, hiring an accountant to help keep the books and prepare tax returns or hiring an attorney to write or review contracts will not make a businessperson out of me. No matter what, I will still need to develop the skills and confidence required for project management and client negotiations. Fortunately, when I asked the experts, "What are the most important skills necessary to be an effective consultant?" they responded that the ability to provide a high-quality work product and exhibit strong interpersonal skills, such the ability to build trust with clients, were more important than business savvy.

Challenged by Questions That Remain

Many components to this process still seem unresolved. Determining fee structures, for instance, still feels like a mystery. So far I have received mixed advice in terms of whether to charge an hourly rate or to put a price on products and other deliverables. Hourly rates I have heard range from $25 to $300. Advice about putting a price tag on deliverables is even more disparate. According to some expert participants, product value should vary depending on what the market can bear, whereas others suggest the price should depend on the added value the product brings to clients, and still others feel the ultimate arbiter has more to do with what both consultant and clients can afford.

Another mystery that remains is how I should market myself. Consultant experts emphasized that their success depended on word-of-mouth advertising, particularly from previously satisfied customers and colleagues in their professional organizations. However, I had heard from only a select sample. I did not speak, for instance, with anyone who had attempted to work as an independent consultant but then found it too difficult or unappealing to continue. Perhaps these missed participants could have answered one of my most pressing questions: How risky is this business anyway? These known challenges and remaining mysteries make me wonder if I need to know more before taking the leap.

Conclusion

After considering my career goals and learning from the experiences of successful professionals, I have a much better idea of the advantages and challenges the world of independent evaluation consulting offers, and I have chosen to proceed with guarded optimism. I am still unsure of what the consulting future holds for me, but I also know that much of my fate in this area is left up to me to construct. I hope and believe that continuing to develop relationships with clients and mentors and continuing to collaborate with those more experienced in the field will eventually help me find my way. I have one more request from this supportive group: Wish me luck!

References

Bellman, G. M. *The Consultant's Calling: Bringing Who You Are to What You Do.* San Francisco: Jossey-Bass, 1990.

Block, P. *Flawless Consulting.* (2nd ed.) San Francisco: Jossey-Bass, 1999.

Edwards, S., and Edwards, P. *Secrets of Self-Employment: Surviving and Thriving on the Ups and Downs of Being Your Own Boss.* New York: Penguin Putnam, 1996.

Lukas, C. A. *Consulting with Non-Profits: A Practitioner's Guide—The Art, Craft, and Business of Helping Non-Profit Organizations and Community Groups Get the Results They Want.* St. Paul, Minn.: Amherst H. Wilder Foundation, 1998.

JUDAH J. VIOLA is a community psychologist at DePaul University and a part-time independent consultant.

4

This chapter examines the stages of growth of six independent consultants, the critical incidents that led to stage change, and training requirements to support this development.

The Evaluation Consultant's Life Cycle: Theory, Practice, and Implications for Learning

Gail V. Barrington

There are many reasons for an individual's choice to become an evaluation consultant, but how does this choice become a lifelong endeavor? Are a consultant's personal and business needs interactive? Do evaluation consultants move through the typical life cycle of an entrepreneur, or does the nature of evaluation work involve a different evolution? What drives practitioners to change over time? Is it the market, the environment, personal choice, or something else? How can we better understand these changes? What kind of learning occurs at each career stage, and how can these learning needs be supported?

Theoretical Overview

Evaluation consultants conduct studies in a variety of organizational settings to assess program effectiveness and efficiency, collecting and synthesizing information, identifying problems, and recommending solutions to improve organizational performance and implement change (Barrington, 2005). They have both academic and practical experience, as well as strong communication, interpersonal, and instructional skills. Living as they do in the interstices between academia and management consulting, it is essential that they model sound research methods and ethical business practice.

NEW DIRECTIONS FOR EVALUATION, no. 111, Fall 2006 © Wiley Periodicals, Inc.
Published online in Wiley InterScience (www.interscience.wiley.com) • DOI: 10.1002/ev.194

Greiner (1998) developed a life cycle model of organizational growth based on a company's development. Each phase begins with a period of evolution followed by steady growth and stability and ending with a revolutionary period of substantial turmoil and change. The resolution of each revolutionary period determines whether the company will move forward to its next stage. Bruce and Scott (1987) created a small business version of this model. They agreed that crisis can be a catalyst for change and suggested it could be precipitated by either internal or external factors. How the manager responded to these key incidents spelled the difference between success and failure in moving the business forward. Their model has five stages: (1) inception, (2) survival, (3) growth, (4) expansion, and (5) maturity.

Cope and Watts (2000) explored the learning process of entrepreneurs and the complex interplay between personal development and that of the firm. While Murphy and Young (1995) suggested that this learning tends to be accidental or unintentional, Greiner thought that each crisis is developmental in nature and provides an opportunity for learning. Cope and Watts (2000) studied six small business owners and determined the critical incidents that had resulted in a stage change. The critical incident technique (Flanagan, 1954) was used to examine these catalysts. Study findings emphasized the complexity of the critical incident concept and demonstrated that entrepreneurs often face prolonged and traumatic critical events that result in fundamental, higher-level learning. They stressed the need for mentoring support programs to help entrepreneurs interpret and reflect on critical incidents so that they can increase the power of their learning outcomes.

Aim of the Research

The purpose of this study was to determine if senior evaluation consultants experienced stages of growth in their practice similar to the small business development stages described by Bruce and Scott, identify the stimuli that led to those changes, determine what the consultants learned from these incidents, and suggest the training that evaluation organizations such as the American Evaluation Association (AEA) could provide to support consultants at different stages.

Methodology

To gain a long enough perspective on life cycle stages, a purposive sample was selected of six senior, nonuniversity-based evaluation consultants. To qualify, individuals were screened for the following criteria: (1) fifteen or more years of experience as an independent evaluation consultant, (2) more than 50 percent of their work based on contracts obtained during that period, and (3) attendance at a minimum of one evaluation conference

NEW DIRECTIONS FOR EVALUATION • DOI: 10.1002/ev

during that period. Names of individuals who were likely to meet these criteria were selected from conference programs of the AEA and the Canadian Evaluation Society (CES) between 1985 and 1990.

Approximately ten names fit the criteria, but not all had current e-mail addresses. An invitation was e-mailed to five individuals, and a sixth was invited in person. The nature of the study and proposed article was described, and an interview guide was provided. All six who were invited agreed to participate. Because two individuals were married to each other, as well as being business partners, they were considered as one participant in the research. Participants' names were changed, and defining features were removed. Nevertheless, they are icons in the field, and some readers may recognize them.

Interviews were conducted either in person or by telephone, and each lasted sixty to ninety minutes. The data were transcribed, mapped for themes, coded, and analyzed. The results were compared to the life cycle stages proposed by Bruce and Scott, and critical incidents were categorized. Other themes that emerged were also explored. While the five life cycle stages defined the research, an additional category, the preinception stage, was added to describe participants' skills, early roles, and predilections that may have led them to or prepared them for a career in independent consulting.

Participant Profiles

Marion has a background in adult education and has been an independent consultant for fifteen years. She also occasionally teaches university courses. She has a staff of three to four individuals and hires subcontractors as needed. Approaching age sixty, she is getting pressure from her family to turn her business over to someone else.

Karen and Mike met while working for the state department of education and discovered that they shared a passion for social justice. They established their consulting business twenty-two years ago, although Karen did not join for the first five years. They have a small support staff and one additional program evaluator. They manage forty to sixty projects a year, from small data entry projects to large international studies.

Charles worked for a regional government for many years and went out on his own in 1986. He has been a sole practitioner ever since, with the exception of a year-long sabbatical. About ten years ago, he relocated his business to Europe and continues to attract a diverse client base.

Nancy moved out of university-based research twenty-one years ago to become a full-time consultant. Her firm actually predated this move as she set it up with several other students "as a lark" while still in graduate school. She has three to four staff members and hires subcontractors as needed.

Brian is the longest-serving independent consultant in the group, with thirty years of experience. Initially he was a partner in a midsized firm, but for the past twenty years has been independent. Many of his clients have been with him for ten to fifteen years. He does no marketing and has more work than he can comfortably handle. His friends say he will never retire.

Ellen has cycled in and out of independent consulting for nearly twenty years. She worked with a partner for four years, then became independent, and later obtained a quarter-time position that she maintained for many years while working on other evaluation contracts. Eventually she took a full-time job, but after four years she returned to her consulting roots. She is currently reestablishing her consulting practice.

Life Cycle Stages

The consultants were able to identify the various life cycle stages they had experienced, allowing some comparisons with the theoretical model proposed by Bruce and Scott. However, it seemed important to understand clearly what drew these people to consulting, to determine if they shared any common characteristics, skills, or predilections. As a result, a preinception stage was added to the model.

Preinception Stage. Two firms were founded by consultants with backgrounds in education and two by individuals with at least one business degree. Two of the six business founders had studied psychology. All but one have a doctorate.

There were some interesting similarities among the consultants in terms of their roles prior to going into business: all had worked in either a government or university setting. Five had already conducted research studies, four had worked on evaluations or needs assessments, and three had been successful grant or proposal writers. Furthermore, they appeared to have a penchant for consulting or applied research, and several reported having a strong need for autonomy in their life. It appeared that for many of them, opening a consulting business was a logical next step.

Inception Stage. Bruce and Scott (1987) describe inception as an individualistic and unstructured stage with a focus on obtaining customers and managing production. How did these consultants get started? In all cases, a critical incident—either external (an economic or political issue) or internal (a significant life event)—prefaced their decision to go into business.

Marion and Nancy worked in university research positions funded by what they called "soft money." Marion was offered a choice: continue her job as a contractor or have no job at all. Nancy was frustrated with the university politics associated with grant writing. The fledgling company she had started as a student was attracting enough work to employ a full-time research assistant, and she decided to join her.

Ellen scanned the political environment and predicted that changes occurring in the national administration would force her boss out of business within two years. It turned out she was right, but long before that, she and an associate jumped ship and started their own partnership.

Brian was tired of managing an evaluation unit for a nonprofit organization and wanted to use his evaluation skills. Having tried consulting on a part-time basis, he was convinced that there was a market for him. Coincidentally he met someone who was looking for a partner. They joined forces and went after "a budding evaluation market."

Charles chose consulting as part of a larger lifestyle change. He was getting married and was unhappy at his government job, so he decided to make both changes at once. When he announced that he was quitting his job, people said, "When you're a consultant, come and talk to me." Within a couple of weeks of his move, he had three contracts.

Mike gave up his government job to get some private sector experience, but soon found that market research and corporate clients did not suit him. He rented a one-room office and purchased a prototype computer. Times were hard, and the bank refused to give him a loan. He had to rely on his retirement savings and credit cards to cover business expenses. Meanwhile, Karen held on to the salary and benefits at her government job.

Survival Stage. Bruce and Scott described business in the survival stage as emergent and fragmented, with a focus on managing revenues and expenses. The consultants spoke of responding to the market in a reactive way, taking whatever work showed up, without planning or direction. Generally this period lasted three to eight years, although Brian found that a hot market and the need for his particular skill set propelled him directly from the inception to expansion stage. Critical incidents formed around external political forces or internal business needs. It was a period of intense learning for them all.

Charles was blindsided by politics. Over an eight-year period, he had worked for twelve different government departments. He was pleased with his diversification. Then a moratorium on government consulting caused many of his contracts to end abruptly. He learned a number of important lessons during this difficult period: (1) the best marketing approach is good work; (2) a reputation for integrity is worth a great deal; (3) even successful projects do not necessarily lead to more work because government clients need to be seen to be fair and to spread out the work; (4) working with a team is a way of lessening the risk; and (5) although client relationships are critical, when the client leaves, his or her replacement may want to make a clean sweep. His advice: "You always have to seek new clients in new markets. You can never really rest on your laurels and be static."

Nancy's experience was remarkably similar. A change in the national administration resulted in changed priorities for social programs. Some of her contracts were cut with thirty days' notice. She summed up the real lesson for her: "One difference between an evaluation business and other service businesses is that [we] are more vulnerable to political sways than others." During this period, Marion and Nancy moved out of their home offices and rented space. For Marion, the separation between work and her private life had become critical. Nancy had six people working for her, and they needed a shared space to foster communication.

Ellen's partnership turned out to be difficult for financial reasons. Although she and her partner had agreed to split the company's income, her partner was bringing in significantly more work than she was, and as a result, their friendship became strained. After four years, they parted company. As economic security issues became paramount, she accepted the quarter-time position that would cushion her for the next thirteen years.

Karen and Mike did not view survival as a stage; it was a constant fact of life:

MIKE: I think [the] reality of the clientele we work with and the nature of our business is that this survival period is constant. It really is, because unlike some of the market research companies, we have huge variation in what we get in terms of projects, and we can't make a lot of money on [them].

KAREN: Our profit margins are very small.

Growth and Expansion Stages. Bruce and Scott describe the growth stage as a time of delegation and new product development, while the expansion stage involves decentralization and system development. Most of the consultants could not distinguish between the two stages. They experienced a growth period of about ten years that was fueled by increased market demand, which led to more business needs associated with office and staff management.

Marion was driven by the market to provide a wider variety of skills. She hired a project manager, some administrative assistance, and subcontractors as needed. After expanding her rented space, she eventually purchased a small house for an office. The business she had described as "accidental" was now very important to her. With the growth of her reputation came lots of work and, with the work, staff management issues.

During this period, Karen finally left her government job and, with trepidation, joined Mike full time. They hired more support staff and relocated their office twice. The market began to drive their business as they won several large contracts. Karen began to travel a great deal, and Mike stayed home to manage the business. Their goal of working together was not being realized.

Nancy also won a large, ongoing contract. Her sales continued to grow, but she kept her staff size to three to four individuals, using subcontractors as needed. It was a happy time for her. She enjoyed watching the work come in and her profits mount.

Brian and his partner had moved directly to the expansion stage. There was a demand for the type of services they offered, and they soon found themselves competing successfully against the large accounting firms of the time. After ten years, they had a staff of twenty-one. Brian could see that research needs were changing and that the economy was unlikely to continue supporting midsized firms such as theirs. He was tired of writing proposals to support the business, and his partner wanted to retire. As a result, Brian went out on his own.

After taking a self-financed sabbatical in Europe, Charles and his wife decided to relocate there permanently. He made some initial contacts with evaluators and potential clients, and within six months, he had his first contract.

Ellen's part-time employment had allowed her to make many contacts in the evaluation community. She mentored a number of evaluators, built capacity, created networks, and fostered evaluation both regionally and nationally. Eventually, however, the part-time work began to taper off, and she relied more and more on getting contracts. With two children to support and health insurance to finance, a new full-time job offer was too good to pass up, and she closed her business.

Maturity Stage. Bruce and Scott characterized maturity as a stage that brought higher dividends and the opportunity for niche marketing. It also brought on the possibility of decline. For most of the consultants, maturity meant having a strong reputation, too much work, and not enough balance in their lives. As Marion commented: "People would say, 'Did you ever realize that this is what it would be like?' And I would say, 'No.' And the thing I think I most wasn't ready for is how it is a 24/7 thing. . . . I used to work hard at any job I had, but it was never so all-consuming as this is." Market demand continued to dominate the businesses, but the consultants were becoming more strategic.

Despite having more than enough work, both Brian and Charles continued to feel marketplace anxiety. They still found it hard to say no to a potential project, because, as Brian put it, "The downside about saying no [to clients is that] . . . evaluation consulting is a performance art and you are only as good as your last dance. . . . If you aren't swimming, if you aren't visible, it would be pretty close to the end of the firm." Karen and Mike experienced a critical incident that had a positive effect on their business. They purchased a photocopier/scanner and no longer needed their data entry staff. With fewer staff, they could downsize their office space. Annual strategic planning sessions helped to remind them of their mission, but, like Marion, they had no separation between work and personal life. However, they had a sense of satisfaction and were enjoying the learning opportunities they would never have experienced in their government jobs. As Mike explained, "We were in eastern Europe doing some work together, and we looked at each other while walking into the marketplace and started laughing. Who would have thought? It has been good, one of the things about the business of evaluation. . . ."

Nancy's business peaked in 2004, and since then she has experienced several critical incidents related mainly to internal management: not marketing far enough ahead with resultant cash flow problems, human resource issues, and an unplanned tax bill. A slow market worsened these setbacks.

NEW DIRECTIONS FOR EVALUATION • DOI: 10.1002/ev

She learned to be more strategic in managing cash flow and subcontracts and more targeted in her marketing approach. Looking down the road, she began to do some succession planning.

Life Cycle Theory Revisited

Overall, the consultants who participated in this study did follow the classic development stages outlined by Bruce and Scott, although the growth and expansion stages tended to blur together. While the consultants' skills, reputations, and businesses grew over time, the development was complex and interactive. Even as mature consultants, their survival through marketing remained their lifeblood, and they saw themselves to be only as good as their previous few projects. As Brian commented, "There is no such thing as linear growth anymore, but a creative destruction and reinvention of yourself. . . . I have gone through ten full cycles and come back to creativity, reinvention, and I am doing that all the time. . . ."

For this group of consultants, the critical incidents they had encountered at various stages had evident patterns. These patterns are summarized in Table 4.1.

At the inception stage, the critical incidents were divided between external political or economic forces (Marion, Nancy and Ellen) and personal preference/lifestyle (Karen and Mike, Charles and Brian). During the survival stage, at least initially, business needs were paramount—whether to get office space (Marion and Nancy) or to deal with financial pressures (Ellen). Charles's critical incident was external and politically induced. During the growth and expansion stages, all of the consultants experienced the external pressures of market demand, resulting in a number of business decisions related to size, staffing, and workload. At the maturity stage, incidents were more mixed, and while market forces (whether increasing or decreasing) continued to be important, other internal pressures related to changing business needs, particularly human resource management, emerged. Personal preference began to reassert itself as a factor. In particular, Charles and Brian chose not to expand, and Karen and Mike, Nancy, and Marion were also considering future directions.

Changing Learning Needs

In their interviews, the consultants made a number of suggestions about their learning needs at different stages of business development. As Nancy commented: "Learning needs? I did have learning needs, and twenty-five years later, I can tell you now what I needed then." The learning needs that the consultants identified having at various stages of growth are summarized in Table 4.2, along with a number of ancillary services they identified as needs as well.

New Directions for Evaluation • DOI: 10.1002/ev

Table 4.1. Critical Incident Analysis

			Study Participant			
Stage	*Marion*	*Karen and Mike*	*Charles*	*Nancy*	*Brian*	*Ellen*
Inception	External: economic	Internal: personal preference	Internal: personal preference	External: political	Internal: personal preference	External: political Internal: personal preference
Survival	Internal: business needs	External: market demand	External: political	Internal: business needs	None	Internal: business needs
Growth and expansion	External: market demand	External: market demand	Sabbatical	External: market demand	External: market demand	External: market demand/decline (quarter-time job)
Maturity	Internal: business needs; External: market demand	Internal: business needs; External: market demand	Internal: personal preference	Internal: business needs; External: market decline	Internal: personal preference; External: market demand	Return to inception stage (full-time job)

Table 4.2. Learning and Service Needs

Life Cycle Stage	Identified Learning Needs	Services Needed
Inception	Marketing/environmental scanning/finding leads	Group health insurance
	Basic business skills, including developing a business plan	Business loans
	Managing cash flow	Used equipment
	Human resource issues—how to hire people or subcontract	
	Business models	
Survival	Business processes	Connections with colleagues to find/expand work
		Evaluation societies
		Evaluation conferences
Growth and expansion	Life balance	IC TIG
	Time management	
	Working with difficult clients	
	Human resource issues—management	
Maturity	Business models	Peer review of project work
	Succession planning/selling your business	Networking opportunities
	Human resource issues—ongoing	Time for reflection

At the inception stage, consultants needed training in marketing and basic business skills such as developing a business plan, managing cash flow, and hiring the right people. Other service needs they identified included access to group health insurance, business loans, and used equipment. As Mike pointed out, the cost of attending conferences was a barrier at this stage.

As they moved through the survival stage, they needed information about good business models and practice. They also wanted to make connections with their colleagues in order to find work or locate subcontractors, and so evaluation conferences and societies became important to them.

During the busy growth and expansion period, they wanted to learn how to achieve a more balanced lifestyle; only Charles was ruled more by personal preference than business needs. They also needed to learn how to manage their time, work with difficult clients, and manage human resources. At this point in their careers, the Independent Consulting Topical Interest Group (IC TIG) was seen an important avenue for meeting colleagues and sharing experiences.

Finally, at the maturity stage, they were still looking for good business models, particularly in terms of succession planning or selling their business. They wanted feedback on their work through peer review processes.

NEW DIRECTIONS FOR EVALUATION • DOI: 10.1002/ev

Networking was still extremely important to them, and they felt a need to reflect on their experiences for deeper learning.

Implications for Professional Organizations

It seems clear that the learning needs of independent consultants vary at different stages of their growth and development. I have had the opportunity to offer an introductory workshop on how to start a consulting business at many AEA and CES conferences since 1993. The content has focused entirely on issues related to preinception (Do I have the right characteristics to be a consultant?) and inception (How do I get started?). Only those interested individuals with enough resources to travel and pay for conference expenses have been able to attend. Someone like Mike would not be able to afford it, yet his needs are just as great. As a result, an opportunity exists for foundations or other funders to support the early training needs of the consultants they may eventually hire by providing travel and training funding or other creative solutions, such as providing training at regional events that are already scheduled for another purpose. Establishing a mentoring and coaching network might be another solution for consultants on limited budgets. The EvalBusiness listserv provides a venue for sporadic support, but the IC TIG could facilitate a mechanism to pair experienced consultants with novices.

During both the survival and the growth and expansion periods, just-in-time learning opportunities such as the Intermediate Consulting Self-Help Fair held at the 2005 joint AEA/CES conference may be an effective training mechanism. Experienced consultants were set up at a number of tables in a large room and provided short training sessions on predetermined business topics, supplying one-page resource summaries, as well as their words of wisdom. Participants selected the topics of interest to them and circulated among the tables in ten-minute intervals. Although this technique is still being pioneered, the fact that it will be offered again at the 2006 conference suggests that it is meeting some of the needs of independent consultants at this stage.

As our profession ages, the learning needs of mature consultants become more urgent. Peer review techniques have already been piloted (Chapter Twelve, this volume) and it is likely that work will proceed within the IC TIG. The topic of succession planning or selling the consulting business has been addressed for the first time in Chapter Five in this volume, which may provide the content for a workshop at an upcoming conference. More challenging are ways of facilitating reflective activities and supporting consultants in their search for lifestyle balance, but the concept of the reflective practitioner is not new (Schön, 1983; Cope and Watts, 2000), and this area warrants training development.

Other Findings

Two final important findings emerged from the interviews. The consultants saw their evaluation organization (whether AEA or CES) as their community, offering them "a fabulous networking and learning opportunity" and fostering the professional contacts they so sorely needed in their busy but lonely lives. The second finding was that these consultants have found many opportunities in their lives to act as mentors, teachers, and leaders. Their record was impressive. Two of them were involved in founding evaluation organizations, and one was instrumental in developing the IC TIG. Several mentioned acting as mentors for other evaluators or sought out teaching roles, developing courses or workshops on evaluation topics. Several also found that presenting at conferences was a way to continue their own learning.

Conclusion

Although only six consultants were interviewed for this study, their experiences resonate with the reality of the field and help to expand our understanding of how consultants grow and change. The interviews also dispelled a common misperception that these evaluation consultants are "in it for the money"; rather, they are driven by a love of applied research, a desire to make a difference in society, a need to teach what they have learned, and a sense of pride in their profession. While retirement may be a vague outline on their horizon, they are in it for the long haul, believing with Ulysses that there is still "something ere the end, Some work of noble note, may yet be done . . ." (Tennyson, 1972). What else can they do? Independent consulting is their life.

References

Barrington, G. V. "Consultants, Evaluation." In S. Mathison (ed.), *Encyclopedia of Evaluation*. Thousand Oaks, Calif.: Sage, 2005.

Bruce, R., and Scott, M. "Five Stages of Growth in Small Businesses." *Long Range Planning*, 1987, 20(3), 40–52.

Cope, J. P., and Watts, G. "Learning by Doing: An Exploration of Experience, Critical Incidents and Reflection in Entrepreneurial Learning." *International Journal of Entrepreneurial Behavior and Research*, 2000, 6(3), 104–124.

Flanagan, J. "The Critical Incident Technique." *Psychological Bulletin*, 1954, 51(4), 327–358.

Greiner, L. E. "Evolution and Revolution as Organizations Grow." *Harvard Business Review*, 1998, 76(3), 55–60, 62–66, 68.

Murphy, H. J., and Young, J. D. "Management and Self-development and Small Business: Exploring Emergent Issues." *Management Learning*, 1995, 26(3), 319–330.

Schön, D. A. *The Reflective Practitioner: How Professionals Think in Action*. New York: HarperCollins, 1983.

Tennyson, A. L. "Ulysses." In H. Gadner (ed.), *The New Oxford Book of English Verse, 1250–1950*. New York: Oxford University Press, 1972.

GAIL V. BARRINGTON *founded Barrington Research Group, Inc., in 1985 in Calgary, Alberta, Canada.*

5

This chapter discusses issues related to succession planning and the valuation and sale of service businesses, with a focus on selling an evaluation business.

Building Your Evaluation Business into a Valuable Asset

Melanie Hwalek, Gregory J. Barber

Determining what will occur with a consulting practice becomes a more pressing concern as an evaluator approaches the age of retirement. Typically independent consultants do not have the pension planning services readily available to evaluators in academic settings, governmental agencies, or large corporations. Without prompts such as automatic pay deductions that are available from human resource departments in larger organizations, evaluation entrepreneurs easily become financially at risk by not giving proper attention to building personal wealth soon enough or well enough. Even with an adequate retirement account, independent consultants may not realize that the service business that they worked hard to establish could put a very golden finish on a preexisting retirement nest egg.

Much has been written about succession planning and about the valuation and sale of service businesses (Business Brokerage Press, 2006; Coltman, 1994; Merfeld and Schine, 2006; Westergard, 2006). This chapter discusses how to arrive at a selling price for an evaluation business. It also describes successful ways to convert an independent consulting practice into a salable and valuable asset.

Putting a "for sale" sign on your business is no guarantee that it will sell. Therefore, it is important for evaluators to know what experts advise about building consulting practices into salable assets and what it takes to successfully sell a service business to a new owner. As this chapter will show, the principles of creating a salable asset apply to both solo entrepreneurs and multiperson organizations.

NEW DIRECTIONS FOR EVALUATION, no. 111, Fall 2006 © Wiley Periodicals, Inc.
Published online in Wiley InterScience (www.interscience.wiley.com) • DOI: 10.1002/ev.195

Unique Aspects of Selling an Evaluation Business

Evaluation entrepreneurs are similar to other professional service companies such as accountants and attorneys but nevertheless differ in significant ways. Like these professionals, owners and managers of evaluation businesses require specialized education and training, rendering the business virtually worthless other than to similarly degreed or trained persons. Evaluation entrepreneurs operate heavily in relationships of trust because customers often only nominally understand the types of services provided. Unlike other professions, however, there is no generally acceptable correct way to do an evaluation because there are standards of accounting and rules to the practice of law. Perhaps the biggest difference between evaluation and other professions is that those who own evaluation businesses seem to value social justice in addition to earning a living.

The unique nature of an evaluation business has both benefits and disadvantages to prospective buyers. On the downside, an evaluation company is the most difficult type of business to sell. Any buyer off the street is not likely to understand the nature of the business and will need some understanding even if he or she does not have the specialized skills needed to perform services for customers. Unlike accounting or law firms, evaluation consultants do not have a prescriptive set of principles and rules based on certification to follow when performing services. In other words, a buyer who is not an evaluator or does not understand what an evaluation is would have difficulty being a successful owner of an evaluation business. This is at the opposite extreme from many salable service businesses, such as a data processing company or transcription service, which require a minimal amount of specialized training to be successful.

On the upside, the market for evaluation services is large and, relative to other professions, the competition small. Although there is no published estimate of the size of the evaluation market, the passage of the U.S. Government Performance and Results Act in 1993 clearly points to the growing need for evaluation services. And comparing the number of evaluators listed in the Yellow Pages with the number of accountants or attorneys would reveal that a typical evaluation customer such as a nonprofit organization would have fewer choices when selecting an evaluator than, say, a financial auditor. Having a large market and limited competition may be attractive to a buyer.

The message for evaluation entrepreneurs is that selling an evaluation business is not easy, but it can be done with the right strategic planning. The key is to make business decisions that lead to increased assets for the company.

Assets of Evaluation Businesses

There are many different ways that a buyer can estimate the value of a business. Hard assets of evaluation companies, such as furniture, equipment, and supplies, have value when the sale is to result in the discontinuance of

NEW DIRECTIONS FOR EVALUATION • DOI: 10.1002/ev

the business. The liquidation value of an evaluation business is not likely to be high because evaluation businesses do not typically have hard assets that would be valuable to a buyer.

More likely, a buyer of an evaluation business will consider the company's earnings, ongoing cash flow, and anticipated future earnings. For an evaluation business, the anticipated value of future earnings is derived from intangible assets. Four types of intangible assets are relevant to evaluation businesses:

- Expertise and history of competent work. The reputation that the company is competent and has a proven history of high-quality work is the largest portion of any consultant's "sales price." When a company is bidding on a contract, for example, its reputation can be the tipping point in selecting it over a competitor. In this sense, the company's expertise and history have value to a buyer.
- Loyal customer base. Having customers who give preference to the company, as evidenced by repeat customers, can provide assurance of future revenues to the buyer. It is important, however, for the customer to be loyal to the company and not only to the business owner.
- Advisers. Having an array of specialists who could be accessed when they are needed broadens the range of services that the company can provide. Typically evaluators have content experts (often subcontractors) who can act as advisers, broadening the array of evaluations that the company can competently conduct.
- Staff and subcontractors. The typical buyer wants to be in charge of the business, with other people doing a major portion of the work. Therefore, having on hand staff who can perform all aspects of an evaluation or subcontractors ready and willing to do different pieces of the work give substantial value to a company.

Cumulatively, these intangible assets comprise the business goodwill. According to Sutton (2003), "From an accounting standpoint it [business goodwill] is the (mathematical) difference between the purchase price and the appraised value of the [tangible] assets" (p.103). Sutton adds, "It is indeed incredible that one of the most common terms involved in buying and selling a business is one of the hardest to pin down" (p. 103).

Although these four intangible assets comprise the core valuables of a service business, there are other ways that evaluation entrepreneurs can increase the selling price of their businesses. Business valuation experts, who are typically hired to value a business in the event of a sale, point to ten ways to increase selling price:

1. Develop proprietary products that make your company unique and desirable to customers. Having products (for example, books, assessment tools) that can be purchased only from your company gives the buyer some

protection from competition and therefore increases the desirability of your business.

2. Develop consumable products or services so that your company is able to draw in repeat customers. Having a service that repeats each year (for example, an annual customer survey and report card) guarantees to the buyer a portion of your sales and profits. This also suggests a lower turnover of customers each year.

3. Turn over some control to a management team in your company. If others understand and can operate part or all of your business, it has more value because the buyer will more quickly be able to maintain business operations after the seller leaves. Even solo practitioners can turn over control, for example, by subcontracting the management of an evaluation to a subcontractor.

4. Consider company size. Larger businesses are often more complex and have a higher risk to the buyer because there is a lot more to manage and control. Smaller companies can be more flexible and can change rapidly as new markets become available (for example, identification of the need for HIV/AIDS interventions) or older markets become obsolete (for example, Web-based access to U.S. Census data reduces the need for census data mining services).

5. Maintain credible financial statements. A clearly understandable financial statement is important to a buyer. The buyer wants to know the finances of your company and how that translates into income and profit for the owner.

6. Develop a broad customer base. The more customers served, the greater the ability of the business to generate a profit year after year. When sales come from only a few customers, the company risks losing a greater proportion of its sales when one of the customers no longer has a need or interest in evaluation services.

7. Steadily increase sales and profits. The buyer wants to know that the business is able to grow continually and bring in more sales. Growth should be at a steady pace that the company is able to handle. For the solo practitioner, this does not necessarily have to translate into increasing the number of employees. Increasing the use of subcontractors can be an alternative way to grow successfully in sales and capacity.

8. Get or stay out of debt. The sales price of a business is decreased by the amount of money that the company owes to lenders. Therefore, getting rid of debt or not adding debt, at least in the five years prior to the sale, increases the value of the business.

9. Serve niche markets. To maintain repeat customers who guarantee future revenues, it is good to have specialized service areas. For evaluators, this could mean specializing in topic areas such as education, aging, or the environment. It could also mean specializing in specific methodologies such as product evaluation or social network analysis. Care should be taken, however, not to be too narrow in specialization. Niche markets for

NEW DIRECTIONS FOR EVALUATION • DOI: 10.1002/ev

evaluators often grow and shrink depending on the political climate. For example, possibly in response to the No Child Left Behind Act passed by the U.S. Congress, the U.S. Department of Education has increased its the demand for certain evaluation methodologies such as randomized control trials. But advocacy efforts to educate politicians about the value of alternative evaluation methods could cause the demand for randomized control trials to shrink.

10. Increase employee or subcontractor incentives. In the evaluation industry, employees and subcontractors are the essence of business operations. Buyers will want some assurance that employees and subcontractors provide high-quality services and that they will continue to work for the new owner. Therefore, it is important to provide incentives for employees and subcontractors that create loyalty to the company.

Knowing what is valued when selling a business and ways to increase the selling price put the evaluator in a position to start planning for a new owner. In business terminology, this is known as succession planning.

Succession Planning

Succession planning is strategizing and implementing what should happen to the business if the owner is no longer there through death or retirement. There is also a subcategory of succession planning, called business continuity planning, that is, planning for when the owner will have a less active role in the business. Either way, there is a transition period during the sale or inheritance of the business in which a new owner learns about business operations in order to take control. In service industries, the transition could last months or even years for the new owner to learn the ropes. Succession planning focuses on increasing the business value and growth in a way that allows the new owner to have enough cash flow and appropriate personnel to weather the transition period. There are five characteristics of effective succession planning:

1. Ensuring that enough cash will be available for the transfer to be easy. Whether the sale is due to death or retirement, cash will be needed to keep the business afloat while the new owner takes the reins of the company. Life insurance is one way to provide cash when a new owner inherits a business. In the case of an owner who is selling the business, easily liquidated assets such as cash, savings bonds, or money market certificates will be needed. Contracts in hand with money owed to the company, referred to as accounts receivable, is another source of immediate cash for the new owner.

2. Identifying, grooming, and gaining commitment from a successor. The selling price for a service business usually comes with assumptions about the future. Perhaps the most prominent contingency is that the

business will continue to achieve the same gross income over a three- to five-year postsales period as it averaged three or five years prior to the sale. If business income declines, so does the selling price of the business. Therefore, it is important that the new owner can quickly take the reins, is acceptable to the current customer base and employees, and is committed to running the business at least as long as the transition period of the sales. If the new owner can be groomed well before the sale, there will be less disruption of business sales or services at the time of the transition.

3. Creating a formal succession plan. The decision that someday the business will be sold to a new owner can happen many years before the sale actually takes place. Therefore, the formal succession plan can take many forms, such as the progressive sale of company stock to employees, leaving the company to a certain person or entity in one's will, or a written sales agreement with a new owner. The more formal the plan is, the easier it is for both the seller and the new owner.

4. Actualizing the succession plan. The best succession plans have a timetable for completion of each major task. This could be as simple as selecting the date when a will is changed so that the new owner inherits all or some of the business in the event of the death of the seller. It can be much more complicated, such as varying the selling price of corporate stock depending on the percentage of the company that others come to own. Every plan has important steps to be carried out, and it benefits the seller and owner to have a specific timetable for succession activities.

5. Reviewing and updating the plan as needed. As time progresses, circumstances change in the personal life of the owner and in the business entity. For example, the owner may no longer have dependent children who would need to be provided for in the case of death. Or as the company matures, new employees or consultants are found, and others are no longer needed or available. These times of change are also times when it is wise to update the succession plan.

The design of the succession plan depends largely on the type of buyer. The sooner the type of preferred buyer is identified, the easier it is for the succession plan to fit the prospective owner's needs.

Potential Buyers of an Evaluation Business

There are three common categories of buyers for evaluation businesses. Each type has advantages and disadvantages:

Employees or Subcontractors. Employees or subcontractors may be interested in purchasing a business because they are familiar with its operations and its customers. Selling to employees or subcontractors allows for the smoothest sales transition because they know the company systems and people. However, employees generally are not well positioned financially and may require the seller to help finance the sale. Furthermore, although

NEW DIRECTIONS FOR EVALUATION • DOI: 10.1002/ev

they may know how to do all aspects of an evaluation, they may not know the financial aspects of running the business. Good workers may prove to be poor managers or financial leaders.

The Competition. Selling to competitors is likely to lead to a smooth transition because, like employees and subcontractors, they are familiar with business operations. The seller should be warned, however, that many competitors may be just "kicking the tires" and not truly intending to buy. Giving a competitor access to customers and billing practices can create losses in the event of a failed sale. Any proprietary methods and systems will lose value when competitors become familiar with them. Also, competitors are best suited to identify weaknesses of the company and know the minimum that can be paid to acquire business practices. After the sale, there could be cultural clashes between the existing practices of the buyers and the practices of the company being bought, which can create unexpected staff and client losses. When the sale is to a competitor, clauses in the sales agreement that value the company based on the seller's continuing to work for a specified period or clauses that price the business based on future revenues become important.

Related Businesses. Businesses such as accounting firms or business consulting companies may be interested in purchasing an evaluation business in order to offer new services and take on new business. By expanding their offerings with services they can easily assimilate, businesses related to evaluation can sell more services to the same or fewer customers with little or no increase in overhead or staffing. There are some pitfalls with related business buyers when there is lack of knowledge and familiarity with evaluation. They may not know, for example, how labor intensive evaluation services can be or may not have staff capable of providing supportive services such as statistical analyses. Selling to a related business, having mature staff, and a supportive infrastructure make for easier transitions and higher sales prices.

Conclusion

According to Sutton (2003), "A buyer is a whole different breed and may not be capable of reproducing your results, nor may he or she want to. What you haven't done holds little or no value to a buyer. If you think changes will increase the value of the company, then do them before the sale" (p. 102).

This chapter provides a road map of changes that evaluators may want to make to their business in order to garner the best price when the day comes to sell, work part time, or have the company run without much of the owner's time or resources. The aspects of selling an evaluation business that are important to a prospective buyer are also outlined.

Selling an evaluation business is a difficult and complicated endeavor. However, it is not impossible. There are many strategies that evaluators can

NEW DIRECTIONS FOR EVALUATION • DOI: 10.1002/ev

implement that are healthy for any evaluation business while simultaneously adding to the sales price of the business in the future:

• Work toward creating systems that are well documented and can be completed by someone other than the owner. This includes systems for managing both the business and the evaluation services. On the evaluation side, for example, have checklists for proposal writing, cost estimating, and data collection. On the business side, have a systematic method for tracking the time spent on each contract and a tickler system for tracking due dates of accounts receivable, with plans in place for sending sixty-day and ninety-day notices of payments due.

• Have a long-range marketing plan, and share it with employees and subcontractors. Keep a watchful eye on market changes so that the long-range plan remains viable. The watchful evaluation entrepreneur will anticipate the impact of public policy and other social and cultural changes on the future market for evaluation services. Social problems that are important to politicians today may be less important when a new federal administration takes office. Having a strategy for staying ahead of the curve will be valuable to a potential buyer.

• Create a customer base that is increasingly dependent on other people in the company to get the job done. When the customer knows only the business owner, it is more difficult for a buyer to retain the customer when the seller leaves. Having other people represent the company to the customer strengthens the value of the business.

• Build a team that will support the business and its eventual sale. This can be done by teaching others the skills of evaluation and delegating work on different contracts to others. Having a large number of employees is only one way to build a team. Having loyal subcontractors can be equally or more valuable to a buyer because using subcontractors makes a company nimble and flexible in responding to market changes. Treat employees and subcontractors well so that they are committed to staying with the company even when the owner leaves or other opportunities for their services arise. Have a trusted attorney and accountant on the team who know the company and can help the buyer and the buyer's attorney and accountant during the valuation and sales process.

• Consider incorporating the business. Solo practitioners may use simple methods of starting their business, such as having an assumed name with no corporate structure. Becoming a corporation allows the business owner to have stock that can eventually be sold in part or in total. Thus, being incorporated opens up more ways to sell the business.

• Educate the valuator. Getting the best price for the business requires that the professional valuing the business is willing to work hard to learn about the evaluation industry. The seller should invest time in teaching the valuator about the potential market for evaluation services and the company's unique strengths in the marketplace. The valuator should also know if the business qualifies as woman owned or minority owned, making it eligible for government contracting set-asides. Alternatively, if the business is not eligible for special consideration, this information should be shared.

• *Start now.* Creating a business that someone else will eventually want to buy takes time. Since valuation experts look back five years in assessing the financial aspects of a business, five years before the sale is the minimum amount of time needed to plan a successful succession. Given that evaluation contracts can last three to five years, building customer loyalty means starting to think about the customer base even longer than five years before the sale. It is never too early to start making business decisions that could eventually create wealth for the owner.

References

Business Brokerage Press. "Rules of Thumb for Valuing Small Businesses." 2006. http://www.bizstats.com/rulesofthumb.htm. Accessed May 12, 2006.

Coltman, M. M. *Buying and Selling a Small Business.* Vancouver, British Columbia: International Self-Counsel Press, 1994.

Merfeld & Schine, Inc. "Business Valuation." 2006. http://www.mergers-acquisitions.com/valu.html. Accessed May 11, 2006.

Sutton, G. *How to Buy and Sell a Business.* New York: Warner Books, 2003.

Westergard, L. "How to Increase Your Company's Value." 2006. http://www.nelsonlambson.com/nlco-articles/cashflowratios.htm. Accessed May 12, 2006.

MELANIE HWALEK is founder and president of SPEC Associates, an evaluation consulting firm in Detroit, Michigan.

GREGORY J. BARBER is a certified public accountant and president of Barber & Associates, CPAs, in Plymouth, Michigan.

6

This chapter offers firsthand experiences in optimizing the organizational and personal dimensions of evaluation research in an independent, entrepreneurial consulting environment.

Entrepreneurial Consulting: Some Structural and Personal Learnings

Morgan Lyons, Maura J. Harrington

We run a small, entrepreneurial applied-research firm of about a dozen employees, and this anecdotal commentary provides a seldom-found opportunity: to talk about ourselves. As senior staff in a business that has lasted more than twenty years, we are eager to share our reflections about what elements of organizational structure have worked best for us and to offer some observations on a personal level as well about how to optimize and remain viable in a volatile professional field.

The term *entrepreneurial consulting* can be applied to an individual, a small firm, or even a quasi-independent unit within a large organization. Wherever it is found, some of its basic features include a capacity to create new work opportunities, to adapt and grow with changing markets, and to deliver quality products and services efficiently. While we give a nod to management and organizational literature, this chapter is primarily about our reflections on the experience of developing and tending our firm.

The general environment of the small and independent applied social research firm can be characterized as ever changing, often unclear, highly competitive, and frequently resource poor. Researchers who survive in this environment must value change and welcome complexity and ambiguity. Although the goals of applied researchers are the same as for any other professional—meaningful work, fulfilling relationships, efficacy, and reward—the route to the entrepreneurial researcher's goals can be turbulent.

Structural Learnings

Our observations are hard won because the risk of failure is always very real, and we in the business do not always get it right. With that in mind, and understanding that "optimal" is highly contextual, we offer advice about how to optimize five essential and intertwined components of the entrepreneurial evaluation research business: staff size, project mix, breadth and depth of expertise, infrastructure, and the organization itself. A lack of optimization in any of these key elements can affect productivity, profitability, and, ultimately, business viability.

Staff Size. The challenge of size is to optimize the number of total staff, number of levels of responsibility, and the relative size of each level. Our organization has varied between five and fifteen employees, and we understand the trade-offs of intimacy versus bureaucracy and balancing staff who do business development, management, and procedural work (Maister, 1993). Each configuration has implications for the kinds of clients and work that can be undertaken. With too few employees, you may not be able to support the overhead of developing new work. The business model for our company has been to use the safety valve of subcontracting other consultants to staff new project teams with appropriate numbers and expertise when the workload becomes too heavy. The upside of external collaboration is immediate capacity; the downside is more difficulty in controlling project operations and quality. There is no simple formula for staff size in relation to project work. Deciding whether to staff up or to outsource can be difficult.

Project Mix. It is important to create a balance of several smaller, more intimate projects with a few larger, high-profile, and more profitable ones. Small projects grossing between ten thousand and thirty thousand dollars are typically more creative and fun in our experience. They provide superior client contact and relationship building and can also function as fiscal fillers that fit into the slower periods of larger projects. However, when a staff researcher is responsible for more than five or six projects, it becomes difficult to maintain priorities and get enough rest. If a set of smaller projects is distributed wisely, the company can benefit from an expanded portfolio and more contacts and references. The employee is stimulated by the variety, and the company can benefit from new business opportunities. In our experience, project mix also affects management needs and profitability, and our error has tended to be having too much fun with too many small projects.

Breadth and Depth of Expertise. Experts give the company a specialist capacity and can build reputation, providing a competitive edge for specialized projects. Having internal expertise in two or three compatible areas does leverage work opportunities, particularly if staff are credentialed with doctorates and publications. However, in a small firm, research generalists provide more flexibility for broad-based marketing. Subcontracting for specialists has worked well for our company. We have managed to do considerable high-quality work in school-related program evaluation without an educator on board, in criminal justice without a criminologist, and in public health without a health professional. The configuration of staff goes to the heart of the kind of business you want to be. To what extent do preferred markets and the current organizational structure support experts or generalists? Our decision has been, "some of each," and the consequence has been opportunity both lost and found.

Infrastructure. Applying just the right amount of staff time on unbillable hours for administration, internal systems development, training, staff meetings, and so on is a constant challenge. Ways to optimize productivity while supporting infrastructure time include setting billable and unbillable goals for each employee in terms of percentage of time used and using tracking systems to monitor time allocation (proposed versus actual). The tracking systems are useful for project billing as well. In our experience, billable goals vary from 90 percent for research support staff to less than 20 percent for administrative staff. In reality, managers find that their billable hours fluctuating wildly from week to week, and so monthly goals may be more appropriate.

Organization. A key question is how to control the chaos and encourage creativity without jeopardizing the entrepreneurial spirit. Complexity theory provides a metaphor for managing in a poorly predictable environment (Rosenhead, 1998). Within bounds, team assignments should be flexible in terms of who leads the project, who does statistical work, and who writes or presents the final report in order to maintain productivity. In this way, the team can respond by shifting roles when a member becomes overloaded, goes on vacation, or is reassigned. However, too little role definition can be a detriment to efficiency and morale. Optimal fuzziness is supported by a good employee handbook, clear but flexible job descriptions, intelligent supervision and appraisal, and the rewards of self-efficacy and remuneration.

Reflections on Strategic Planning. Perhaps the most poignant conclusion we have come to is that strategic planning is likely to be worthless for the long term (that is, two to three years) but essential for the short term (that is, the next few months). This may seem like a startling comment from a firm that does strategic planning consulting, but how much to plan ahead and how much to be ready to respond to contingencies, both our own and those of our clients, is a defining question for entrepreneurial consulting.

Personal Learnings

Managing employee expectations and comfort levels is intimately related to structure. Quite outside the employee handbook, the social contract between the company and the employee is personal and thus perceived differently by each employee. Employees' feelings about opportunity, equity, and entitlement, as well as their anxieties, vary widely. Key learnings relate to when talent arrives, when talent leaves, intangibles, time off, and handling growth.

When Talent Arrives. Candidate interviews and early employee orientation can do only so much to ensure that employee skills and expectations match company requirements. Just as burnout can challenge the employee, burn-in challenges the organization, and the extra time required to orient and train new staff has to fall under the category of unbillable hours. Sometimes assumptions about a new employee's research skills are inaccurate, and unanticipated training, coaching, or reassignment may result. Becoming acculturated to the company's way of work is needed for every new employee, even those who have worked in a similar type of consulting company. It is a happy result when the new talent is so good that business needs to be generated rapidly to take advantage of the employee's skill set and reinforce his or her decision to join the firm. New talent is generally disruptive, but it is a good problem.

When Talent Leaves. The typical stay of employees in a small, independent research firm is perhaps three to five years, but it takes one to two years to learn the business, even if the employee already has the requisite research and client relations skills. Once employees are seasoned, they help to build the business through attracting projects and building close, unique external relationships. These can be endangered when the employee leaves, even if the departure is friendly. If two or more departures happen simultaneously, the loss can seriously threaten a small organization. Critical projects may be lost or damaged, and the morale of remaining staff, including perceived insecurity, can also become a threat. Reasons for staff departure vary, but each must be explained to remaining staff to ease the loss and shift the focus to moving forward together. With determination, regrouping works very well.

Intangibles. If there is no coffee boutique next door, the office needs to have a friendly kitchen with a high-end coffee pot. Other ways to build positive office atmosphere include providing quiet places for work and flexible systems to make those work spaces either warm or cool, light or dark for office mates with diverging preferences. A budget for personal art, space heaters, orthopedic chairs, and footrests signals caring. Relationships are what it is about, and so time and space are required for casual chatting and laughter, unscheduled fun breaks, and catered lunches—all reasons to get to work and to work efficiently. A significant investment in an architecturally friendly build-out a few years ago has made our work environment a highlight of the business.

Time Off. Job demands in the entrepreneurial firm can cause some employees to put off their vacations indefinitely, resulting in huge accounts payable for unused vacation. Concurrent deadlines and pop-up proposal opportunities can also subvert an employee's much-needed time off. The cell phone and the Internet entice us to trade personal renewal time for professional efficacy. The company may benefit, but only in the short term. How consuming the job becomes is individual in nature and depends on personal work ethic, family pressures, and stamina. There may be no better palliative than remembering to thank employees for their valor and encouraging them to have a good weekend or to be sure to get out of town.

Handling Growth. The happiest anxiety for small firm management is a huge growth opportunity that requires hiring several new staff, shifting established and functional responsibilities, and floating expenses until the new client can pay the first large invoice. The most serious consequence of a big growth opportunity may relate to expectations for continuity on the part of both staff and the client. Job expectations may need to be renegotiated. If résumés of current staff were submitted in the proposal and those individuals are currently overloaded, negotiations regarding project staffing may be in order with the new client as well. Most troublesome is the realization that increased revenues can mean a decrease in profits if staff expect that their personal incomes will grow along with the company's.

A Note on Information Technology

Significant investment in information technology (IT) is an expensive requirement, and the bar continually rises. An informative, attractive, and easily navigated Web site is essential to make a good first impression. Clients, as well as potential employees and partners, often go there first to determine what it would be like to do business with you. Do you serve nonprofits and their communities? Can you work with multicultural clients? Can you take on both large and small jobs? Are your evaluation methods rigorous? Your entrepreneurial spirit will also show.

Inside the shop, information systems for communications as well as for production are critical. In our proposals, we often advertise that we have state-of-the-art hardware and software, are internally networked, are online, have powerful processing capacity, and can produce attractive full-color reports. We budget for an on-call computer service vendor as well as for staff training for software proficiency. Although we may outsource large production jobs and or the manipulation of huge data sets, basic research functions such as creating databases and conducting qualitative analysis are done in-house. Employees' remote access to company e-mail and a cell phone is essential (although our employee handbook prohibits using the phone while driving). IT supports productivity, but it can be exhausting as well. Midnight e-mails and business calls on vacation attest to its addictive nature, and optimizing it is an ongoing challenge.

Conclusion

Our comments represent the wisdom we have gained over a couple of decades of practice. Nevertheless, they are tentative at best because both the

NEW DIRECTIONS FOR EVALUATION • DOI: 10.1002/ev

macro and micro environments for independent, entrepreneurial consulting keep changing. For senior staff who have been around awhile, employees get younger and younger, as do our clients and colleagues. New markets like homeland security and new funder requirements like the current outcomes focus keep our business near the edge of chaos. So why do it? The answer is something akin to the mountain's "being there" for a climber. Wealth and popularity are unlikely for the small research business. Perhaps the best reasons to sign on are if you have a short attention span and need stimulation, if you love an intense puzzle-solving enterprise in the company of fine colleagues, or if you find fulfillment by helping service organizations do their good works better. If these describe you, as they do us, we highly recommend it.

References

Maister, D. H. *Managing the Professional Service Firm.* New York: Free Press, 1993.
Rosenhead, J. "Complexity Theory and Management Practice." 1998. http://human-nature.com/science-as-culture/rosenhead.html. Accessed November 15, 2005.

MORGAN LYONS is president of Lodestar Management/Research in Los Angeles, California.

MAURA J. HARRINGTON is senior researcher and vice president of Lodestar Management/Research in Los Angeles, California.

7

This chapter explores how and why independent evaluation consultants form collaborative relationships with each other.

Collaborative Relationships in Evaluation Consulting

Stephen C. Maack, Jan Upton

"It is remarkable how much our culture is fascinated by the idea of the loner. The figure of the sole pioneer or solitary adventurer is an integral part of our nation's history and folklore. . . . But when we peel away the layers of idealism surrounding this image, we discover that no major achievement is accomplished alone" (Lonier, 1994, p. 323). People are often driven to become "independent" as part of the desire to go out on their own. Independent evaluation consultants, however, frequently collaborate with others on evaluation projects. This chapter explores such collaborative relationships from both sides: those leading evaluations with subcontracted consultants and those who work as subcontractors.

The two of us met when Stephen contacted Jan for an informational interview in fall 2002. Jan ran a sole proprietorship comparable to the one Stephen was planning. Both of us have continued to collaborate regularly with each other, as well as with others. Although in some ways our relationship is unique (we have never met in person despite working together on projects since 2003), we have come to realize through our interactions with other consultants that collaboration is pervasive. Working with others offers a wide variety of potential benefits for consultants at different stages of their careers. For newer consultants, it provides an avenue of obtaining initial contracts and learning from more experienced consultants. For those more experienced, it is often an essential business management strategy.

NEW DIRECTIONS FOR EVALUATION, no. 111, Fall 2006   © Wiley Periodicals, Inc.
Published online in Wiley InterScience (www.interscience.wiley.com) • DOI: 10.1002/ev.197

Theoretical Context

A variety of disciplines have written about professional collaboration within and among organizations since the mid-1960s. The theoretical basis for cooperative strategy has largely come out of economics and sociology (de Rond, 2003). Another body of literature from career development and organizational human resources covers such matters as individual skills development, using new technology for communication (Schrage 1990), cultivating communities of practice (Wenger, McDermott, and Snyder, 2002), teamwork, and managing distribution of labor among professionals. However, little has been written about collaboration that is specific to independent evaluation consulting except as it relates to firms starting up (Lonier, 1994) or project management (Kemp, 2006). Summarizing the various theories and how they relate to the data we collected is beyond the scope of this chapter. Following de Rond (2003), we feel that no overarching theory is available that would fully explain the variety in our small, nonrandom sample.

Methodology

We developed a brief survey about collaborative relationships that we advertised on the following listservs: the American Evaluation Association's (AEA) Independent Consulting Topical Interest Group (46 percent of respondents), AEA's Multiethnic-Issues Topical Interest Group (18 percent of respondents), and the Evaluation Anthropology Topical Interest Group (10 percent of respondents). Members of these lists were also encouraged to invite others who might be interested to contribute (6 percent of respondents). Twenty percent of respondents did not indicate how they heard of the survey. Ninety-four consultants completed the survey (see Table 7.1).

The survey included basic questions to respondents about their experience as consultants, business structures, and collaborative relationships. We also asked participants to give examples that described ways they had partnered with others and emphasized our interest in efforts intended to increase diversity. We encouraged consultants to tell us stories about their experiences with collaboration and allowed commonalities, concerns, and definitions to emerge from their writings. Results from the convenience sample provide rich insights about how independent evaluation consultants work and collaborate with each other. Statistical results reflect only this particular self-selected group, but the findings are a starting place in providing an understanding of the importance of collaboration and can help inform future research efforts. Fifty-seven people (61 percent) shared one or more stories.

Collaboration Experiences of Survey Respondents

Although 70 percent of the respondents had no employees, the data support the experience that many in the AEA Independent Consulting Topical Interest Group have expressed informally: being an independent consultant does

Table 7.1. Description of Respondents

	Number	Percentage
Years of experience as an independent evaluation consultant		
Less than 1 year	4	4
1–5 years	29	31
6–10 years	30	32
11–19 years	20	21
20 or more years	11	12
Operate a home-based business		
No	27	29
Yes	67	71
Number of employees		
None	66	70
1–2	13	14
3–4	7	7
5 or more	8	9
Ever had a subcontracting or partnership with another consultant or business		
No	15	16
Yes	76	84
Number of collaborations in the past year		
None	15	16
1–2	46	49
3–4	17	18
5 or more	13	14
No response	3	3
Ever subcontracted or partnered with a specific consultant or business out of desire to increase diversity		
No	38	40
Yes	50	53
No response	6	7
Think you or your company has ever been asked to join a project as part of increasing diversity of an evaluation team		
No	49	52
Yes	40	43
No response	5	5
Total	94	100

not necessarily mean working solo. Lonier (1994) lays out three staffing options for small businesses: partner with other entrepreneurs, build a flexible staff with part-time help, or hire full-time employees. About 14 percent of survey respondents had one or two employees, 7 percent employed three or four, and 9 percent had a staff of five or more. While one might expect firms with more employees to have less need for subcontracting, this was

NEW DIRECTIONS FOR EVALUATION • DOI: 10.1002/ev

not the case; 93 percent of the organizations with three or more employees had engaged in subcontracting relationships at some point.

A high 84 percent of all respondents had had one or more collaborative relationships in the past year. Although the small sample size precludes reliable chi-square results, there was a strong, positive correlation of firm size with number of collaborations in the past year. About 79 percent of firms with three or more employees had at least three collaborations in the past year, compared to 46 percent of those with one or two employees and 20 percent of those with no employees. The most frequent response was one or two collaborations in the past year for independent consultants with one or two employees (39 percent) or no employees (61 percent). Independents often collaborate no matter what their firm size, and larger firms collaborate more often. The following sections discuss the reasons that evaluation consultants work together and some of the differences based on experience. We then highlight the common aspects of effective collaborations, the potential pitfalls, and our findings regarding diversity.

Reasons for Collaborating. Evaluation consultants gave many reasons for collaborating. Busy sole proprietors and consultant firms brought in subcontractors to help manage workload during busy periods or as part of growing the business. They also often had a need for specialized and complementary skills—for example:

- Statistics and research design
- Qualitative research
- Experience with a specific ethnic group
- Experience with a content area, such as elementary or higher education
- Verbal and written abilities in a particular language
- Experience developing and administering online surveys

Respondents referred to this as skills diversity. Several minority respondents described their experience of being asked to join certain project teams as "representatives of diversity." One explained, "The organization needed a consultant who could provide content expertise as well as representation as a member of an underserved ethnic population." Some nonminority respondents similarly noted use of ethnically diverse collaborators.

Additional reasons for collaborations included:

- Need for local on-site consultants to attend meetings and do on-site observations and in-person interviews
- Need to reduce costs (entry-level people or newer consultants are useful for this purpose)
- Subcontracting to local companies required by client

NEW DIRECTIONS FOR EVALUATION • DOI: 10.1002/ev

- Large projects, especially those with multiple sites
- Opportunity to work on interesting projects
- Reduction of isolation for single consultants
- "Having two heads" is better than one for creatively thinking through project issues
- Way to meet deadlines

We add two of our own reasons to this list:

- Increasing objectivity, especially when a consultant has a long-term relationship or multiple projects with a client
- Opportunity to select colleagues with whom one wants to work on a project because of respect, admiration, personal liking, or a prior relationship

Less Experienced Evaluators. Typically those who had been consultants for five years or less were brought in by others. This was the case for ten of the sixteen respondents (63 percent). Some specifically sought to develop their skills through collaborating with others. Subcontracting was also a way to develop a new consulting business. More senior consultants recognized or sought collaboration with junior consultants who have either complementary or supplementary skills. In some cases, the novice had a prior relationship with a client that the more senior consultant recognized as an advantage for successful completion of the project.

Moderately Experienced Consultants. The seventeen respondents with stories who had six to ten years of experience had a greater mixture of types of collaborative relationships and were more nuanced in their discussions of these relationships. Text analysis shows that 53 percent spoke primarily of being subcontractors to someone else. However, 29 used subcontractors, and 18 percent mentioned both kinds of situations. This group had similar reasons for subcontracting their services to others as those with less experience did: they were selected mainly for their specialized skills, being an ethnic minority, or simply knowing how to do evaluation.

Having been in business for themselves longer, these independent consultants mentioned a wide range of subcontracting terms: one month to ten years. Longer-term relationships often fell in the category of repeat business. Of course, initially, these now more experienced consultants were novices who had begun to build up what would eventually become long-term collaborative consulting arrangements.

Moderately experienced consultants who hired others as subcontractors more clearly stated what they were seeking and how they wanted the relationship to operate than those newer to consulting. The ability to recognize specific subcontracting terms and think these were important enough to mention on a survey may signify more extensive experience. Even when acting as subcontractors, this group appeared to have more input into the work arrangements and relationships.

More experienced evaluators had learned how to negotiate the nature of the collaboration. They had the confidence and sufficient power to insist on certain conditions. There were also more instances of individuals' cowriting proposals and switching off on who took responsibility as the lead evaluator. These consultants specifically mentioned evaluation skills more frequently.

Very Experienced Consultants. We include in this category fourteen consultants with eleven to nineteen years of experience and nine with twenty or more years of experience. One-third of the stories came from very experienced consultants. Only four (17 percent) in this group specifically mentioned being subcontractors themselves. The details they provided indicated work requiring advanced evaluation skills, often on large projects in lead roles.

Indeed, it was typical of the remaining nineteen very experienced consultants (83 percent) that they had brought in the business, landed the contract, and, when it was large or multiyear or required specialized skills, they would bring in subcontractors to help. Sometimes this let the very experienced consultants concentrate on work for which they were especially well suited. In other cases, it made the contract more competitive because less expensive subcontractors could handle a portion of the work.

Several in this group spoke of long-term relationships with subcontractors, including some who had become friends. We similarly have become good friends—an unintended, delightful consequence of what started as a purely business collaboration. Some respondents made a concerted effort to bring along newcomers and deliberately sought long-term relationships with subcontractors. One of the respondents noted:

> I have had my own business since 1994. Starting about 1997, I started getting so much business that I asked people to work with me as independent consultants. Right now I have five people working with me: one for almost ten years, one for seven years, one for six years, and one for one year. In general, two of us have a better quantitative background, and three are more qualitatively oriented. All but one are very good writers. All have become personal friends as well as collaborators. . . . I am the lead evaluator for those projects—design the evaluation, handle the budget/invoices/payment, assign tasks in collaboration with the consultants.

One striking aspect of the stories of the very experienced consultants was the extensive variety of expertise they put together, as well as the arrangements made with the teams and the clients. Having the confidence and skill to assemble and be responsible for teams that include subcontractors is an intimidating prospect for some people. Working into that level of self-confidence may take time and experience. It requires being willing to admit that one might not have all the skills needed for a project or that a client might be better served by bringing in someone else. It also requires managing other people, something that those who have not previously been supervisors in "regular" jobs might not have had experience doing. The more people who are involved, the harder this is—and with larger, longer-term projects, very experienced consultants often have several people involved on one project or on several projects at once. One consultant, in a frank self-reflection, put it this way:

> I contracted with another consultant because I had the skills for most of the job but felt I was weak in this certain area. My options in the past have been to not go after or take the job or just blunder my way through it. Perhaps *blunder* isn't the right word because in the past, clients have been anxious to hire me and don't seem to have the concerns I have about quality. . . . I have the experience and confidence now—after thirteen years of consulting to put together a team of my own to ensure quality and good working conditions.

Collaboration Challenges

Some consultants gave examples of collaborations that did not go as smoothly as they would have liked. They generally attributed the problems to their inexperience with such arrangements and noted they have since learned ways to avoid future pitfalls. As a result, they emphasized the need to define more carefully the specifics of the collaborative relationship on new projects. Conflicts over individual responsibilities and budget could be particularly contentious:

> After out-of-pocket expenses, we split the money three ways. This was done in equal shares (33–33–33 percent) up until the time that one partner experienced a personal crisis and was needed more at home. At that point the money was split 40–40–20 percent. I have to say that I eventually resented the split, given how much more time and expertise I contributed to the accomplishment and quality of the work. . . . I did it for the professional camaraderie and in hopes of improving the quality of my work, which didn't pan out. . . . I don't think I would do it again. I continue to collaborate with subcontractors, but I am in the driver's seat and I pay them by the hour. And I only subcontract with other professional evaluators.

> It works very well until a client doesn't pay on time and I am left with someone (a friend) who is looking to get paid. This is by far the biggest drawback . . .

Jan has learned to do a test of compatibility by initially doing short-term, low-commitment contracts with new subcontractors.

Collaborative activities especially likely to run into problems occurred when the client or a larger evaluation firm selected evaluation team members and the consultants did not previously know each other or had not

NEW DIRECTIONS FOR EVALUATION • DOI: 10.1002/ev

worked with one another before. Working with unknown people was most problematic when the work styles were not a good match or the product quality did not meet the lead consultant's standards. As professionals, respondents involved in such projects might make them work, but such collaborations were somewhat less comfortable, as one explained: "Several times in the past, like ten years ago, I worked with 'teams' put together by the client. For example, they chose three consultants for three different components of the same project and said, 'Work together.' Once, in a small project, the roles were fairly clearly defined, but it was a horrible experience because we really didn't work as a team."

Another dissatisfaction with working on a large project was the lack of control over certain aspects of the research, such as timing of data collection and reports. One respondent explained her frustrations with subcontracting: "Sometimes it's hard not to be an equal partner—I find myself performing specific tasks without an overall picture of the project we're evaluating." Consultants learned from their errors, and most handled these practical and essential aspects through a contract or memorandum of understanding covering division of effort, billing, and subcontract arrangements—and how to handle matters if collaborations go sour and need to be dissolved. It is clear from the high level of collaboration that although a few had unpleasant experiences, they were continuing to work with others—with more deliberation in their contractual arrangements and, if at all possible, in control so that they could select partners they knew and trusted.

Aspects of Effective Collaborations

Lonier (1994, pp. 318–319) identifies seven characteristics (integrity, upbeat personality, reliability, skills, complementary ability, similar values, and compatible communication styles) that "solo entrepreneurs say they look for when choosing others to work with them." Survey respondents similarly highlighted these as aspects of effective collaborations. They additionally placed great emphasis on "trust," "mutual respect," "complementary ways of thinking," and consistent production of "quality work." We add the importance of "complementary writing styles."

Related to these values, most respondents indicated that initial contact with their collaborators had taken place before they began to work together. Consultants especially tended to bring former coworkers or mentors or mentees into projects when their workloads grew too large or they needed a specialized skill set for a project. Some had maintained a collegial relationship or friendship with these people for quite some time (as much as twenty years or more). One respondent elaborated on this phenomenon:

> Collaborations with some consultants can last many years, and even across concurrent or sequential projects. . . . . Collaboration is a standard and important

business practice for us. Collaborators are typically well known through past working, volunteer, or personal relationships. Thus, they tend to work very well. It is good business, and it is professionally stimulating. We will definitely continue to contract out and to subcontract with selective professionals and firms who expand our capacity to perform and improve our networking and reputation.

Collaborating for Diversity

Although our data provide only a preliminary glance, half of the respondents had brought in others to projects as part of expanding their diversity (defined as skills diversity), and almost as many had been asked to participate in a project partly because of their race or ethnicity. Both of us have similarly had client requests for "representative" consultants or deliberately sought out ethnically diverse evaluators to strengthen teams, especially in projects that include a focus on minority populations. However, as respondents emphasized, one's research and writing skills are essential. Although representative evaluators may be sought initially on the basis of race/ethnicity, they must first and foremost have the experience and abilities needed to fulfill project requirements. One very experienced consultant wrote: "I am black, so it is not unusual for people to seek me out to 'represent' or to enhance project diversity. This has happened many times, but at this stage in my career, people invite me for my reputation first."

A few of the minority respondents also described the personal, cultural, and professional value of "protecting" the groups they represent. One clarified:

> I did it to preserve and protect tribal sovereignty and self-determination. Evaluation, like land or gaming rights, is a federally protected aspect that Indians have a legal right to. I'd do this again because "outsiders" often come in during research and evaluation projects and do not conduct themselves in an ethically, culturally, or scientifically appropriate way. My role is a gatekeeper, translator (across/between tribes and funders), and capacity builder for Natives and non-Natives where evaluation is concerned.

Several consultants who mentioned diversity emphasized the match of their personal goals with the larger group. Another explained that her efforts were to help disadvantaged nonprofit groups get research funding and expand their capacity.

There is a high demand for representative evaluators, and collaboration is one way of bringing more diversity into projects. However, more needs to be done to facilitate access to consultants with needed professional skills as well as specific personal characteristics. It is clear that independent evaluation consultants learn over time to seek out and maintain contact with those

NEW DIRECTIONS FOR EVALUATION • DOI: 10.1002/ev

with whom they think they might like to work in the future. More research on this topic might explore additional needs of less experienced, moderately experienced, and experienced consultants, minority and nonminority. In particular, it is important to explore the tools and approaches that would allow more systematic consultant matching and mentoring beyond the informal processes currently in place.

References

de Rond, M. *Strategic Alliances as Social Facts: Business, Biotechnology, and Intellectual History*. Cambridge: Cambridge University Press, 2003.

Kemp, S. *Project Management Made Easy*. Madison, Wisc.: Entrepreneur Press, 2006.

Lonier, T. *Working Solo: The Real Guide to Freedom and Financial Success with Your Own Business*. New York: Portico Press, 1994.

Schrage, M. *Shared Minds: The New Techniques of Collaboration*. New York: Random House, 1990.

Wenger, E., McDermott, R., and Snyder, W. M. *Cultivating Communities of Practice: A Guide to Managing Knowledge*. Boston: Harvard Business School Press, 2002.

STEPHEN C. MAACK *is the owner and lead consultant of REAP Change Consultants in Los Angeles, California.*

JAN UPTON *is the president of Institutional Research Consultants in Columbus, Ohio.*

NEW DIRECTIONS FOR EVALUATION • DOI: 10.1002/ev

8

This chapter reviews the literature on partnerships, along with examples from the field, to offer a model for the evolution of effective, collaborative evaluator-client relationships.

Client Relations: More Than Just "Business"

Courtney L. Malloy, Patricia A. Yee

In our roles as evaluators, we have worked with a variety of clients, from single researchers to government agencies, from community-based organizations to commercial service businesses, from school districts to multibillion-dollar companies. We have worked with clients on projects lasting only one week and others for as long as sixteen years. What we have learned in our firm's twenty-five years of operation is that our success in the field of evaluation depends just as much on cultivating effective client relationships as it does on our skills and expertise. We have also learned that when we approach our client relationships as collaborative partnerships, we produce more effective evaluations and enjoy more professionally rewarding experiences.

In this chapter, we review the literature on partnership evolution to offer strategies for developing collaborative evaluator-client relationships. We begin with a brief introduction to partnerships and our approach to client relationships. A synthesis of the literature on partnership evolution is provided and applied to the evaluator-client relationship. We conclude with recommendations that can be used to nurture effective partnerships in the field of evaluation.

Defining Partnerships

Based on the benefits of collective action, partnerships are groups of organizations voluntarily working together to solve problems of mutual concern

and accomplish common goals. According to Gray (1989), partnerships offer mechanisms through which "parties who see different aspects of a problem can constructively explore their differences and search for solutions that go beyond their own limited vision of what is possible" (p. 5). The research literature is rich with examples of organizations coming together to solve problems and address organizational improvement concerns. Collaboration among organizations has occurred for decades in the fields of construction, publishing, film and recording, textiles, and the aircraft industry (Powell, 1990). Partnerships have been documented in a variety of policy areas, including education, conservation, welfare reform, public health, transportation, and prison management (Dunn, 2000; Kamieniecki, Shafie, and Silvers, 2000; Rom, 2000; Rosenau, 2000; Schneider, 2000; Sparer, 2000; Wohlstetter, Malloy, Smith, and Hentschke, 2004b).

Partnerships have been termed interorganizational relationships (Oliver, 1990; Ring and Ven, 1994; Robertson, 1998), strategic alliances (Austin, 2000; Gulati, 1995; Kanter, 1994), and networks (Powell, 1990). They are typically voluntary, enduring relationships that involve resource sharing and joint decision making.

Our most satisfying experiences with clients result when we approach the relationship as an evolving partnership. We attempt to move beyond the contractual business relationships that consultants have with their clients (that is, vendor-consumer) to a place of partnership where we share resources and work collaboratively to gather information, answer critical questions, make decisions, and solve problems. These clients view us as integral members of their team, invested in their success; we see them as partners who contribute numerous assets to the evaluation process.

The Evolution of Evaluator-Client Partnerships

From the literature, we know that effective partnerships progress through several phases as they evolve and mature (Austin, 2000; Bardach, 1998; Child and Faulkner, 1998; Coe, 1988; Gray, 1989; Oliver, 1990; Waddock, 1989; Wohlstetter, Smith, and Malloy, 2005). A partnership is initiated when an individual or organization has a specific need that stimulates the search for a partner. Next, the work of the partnership begins; formal meetings occur and collaborative structures emerge. A partnership matures when stakeholders begin to evaluate their successes and challenges. Drawing on Waddock (1989) and Wohlstetter, Smith, and Malloy (2005), our synthesis and application of the literature on partnership evolution is organized into three distinct phases: initiation, operations, and evaluation (Figure 8.1).

Initiation. During the initiation phase, the structures and processes of a partnership are informal as participants begin to learn about each other and develop the purpose for the endeavor. Research has uncovered a number of conditions that facilitate the initiation of effective partnerships, including complementary needs and assets, compatible goals, and trust.

Figure 8.1. The Evolution of Partnerships

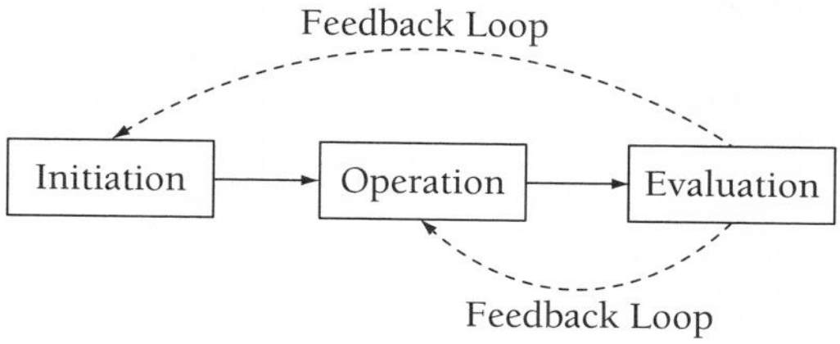

Feedback Loop

Initiation → Operation → Evaluation

Feedback Loop

Complementary Needs and Assets. Organizations often decide to partner not because they have the same needs but because they have complementary needs and assets (Austin, 2000; Child and Faulkner, 1998; Kanter, 1994; Oliver, 1990; Robertson, 1998; Waide, 1999; Weiss, 1987; Wohlstetter, Malloy, Smith, and Hentschke, 2004a). Organizations often require additional financial resources to begin, enhance, or significantly innovate programs, which require them to seek a new partner. In some instances, organizations benefit politically by gaining greater credibility or legitimacy from well-established partner organizations. Other organizations establish collaborative arrangements in order to meet necessary legal or regulatory requirements that could not have been met without an appropriate partner. Finally, partnerships are often initiated to meet organizational needs and work more effectively toward accomplishing strategic missions. Through an effective partnership, an organization may find new ways to increase efficiency and productivity. Moreover, organizations are often able to solve problems more effectively with the aid of a partner because greater capacity is bought to bear on issues of concern (Weiss, 1987).

The reasons underlying the initiation of an evaluator-client relationship vary. The client may need an evaluator to meet a requirement from a funding agency or government entity. In other instances, the client seeks an external evaluator as one way to enhance the credibility and legitimacy of an evaluation process for stakeholders. Clients also initiate relationships with evaluators to increase their efficiency and productivity: they seek information that can be used to improve organizational or program performance. Some organizations need assistance with program monitoring activities because they lack the requisite resources to accomplish the task on their own. Finally, in a few cases, we have initiated partnerships with clients because they bring unique resources that we do not have. For example, we have partnered with clients because they have special expertise or access to targeted populations in order to be more competitive for funding awards.

It is important to note that for an evaluator-client relationship to evolve into a partnership, complementary needs and assets must be present. That is, the relationship is not one-sided, wherein only the evaluator offers capacity and expertise to accomplish the evaluation. The evaluators may indeed

NEW DIRECTIONS FOR EVALUATION • DOI: 10.1002/ev

be hired because they possess assets—evaluation skills and expertise—that can meet the client's need for an evaluation. However, to nurture a true partnership that will last over time, the evaluator must view and approach the client as a partner who also brings essential assets to the relationship. Clients have the potential to contribute more than just the financial resources required for the evaluation. They are also often the content experts; they know the most about their organization, their program, and their stakeholders. Moreover, the client can broker relationships with key stakeholders that are essential to accomplishing evaluation activities, such as data collection and report dissemination. When the evaluator-client relationship is not viewed as one in which both the evaluator and the client have complementary needs and assets, there is little hope that a long-lasting partnership will evolve.

Compatible Goals. Critical to the successful initiation and evolution of a partnership are compatible goals that may not be achieved otherwise (Austin, 2000; Das and Teng, 1998; Kanter, 1994; Oliver, 1990; Robertson, 1998; Spillett, 1999). For an evaluator-client relationship to evolve into a partnership, it is essential that both the client and the evaluator clearly understand the purpose of the evaluation and have compatible views of what the evaluation can achieve. Furthermore, both must view the relationship and the product of the relationship—the evaluation—as necessary and beneficial. This is often challenging in instances when the client is mandated to seek out an evaluator. There can be resistance to losing a portion of program funding to an evaluator as well as fear that future program funds will be lost due to evaluation findings. In some cases, clients do not deem the evaluation necessary or useful and see it only as another form of regulation and bureaucracy. In these instances, the client is often most concerned with producing an evaluation that will be viewed favorably by a funding agency, which is in direct conflict with the goal of the evaluator to produce a high-quality, objective evaluation. In these cases, we attempt to introduce our clients to the value of evaluation and help them see the benefits of the process for program improvement. We also point out that evaluations are needed to show the positive effects of their hard work and dedication. Such an approach encourages the client to view the goals of the evaluation in a different light and move beyond thinking about the evaluation as merely an accountability-driven process.

Trust. Finally, trust is needed to facilitate the initiation of partnerships; without a mutual willingness to work together, the relationship is unlikely to evolve. Initial trust in partnerships is often established through existing networks and relationships (Austin, 2000; Waddock, 1989; Waide, 1999). Much of our evaluation work, for example, has grown by word of mouth. New clients often come to us by referral; someone they trust has told them about our work and recommended us. Other clients hear about us through reputable networks that we belong to (for example, the American Evaluation Association or the California Association of Homes and Services for the Aging).

Robertson (1998) suggests that open communication, shared values, and mutual respect among partners increase the interorganizational trust that is required to sustain a partnership. We have learned over time that in order to develop and maintain effective partnerships with clients, we must listen to them; respect their points of view, culture, and experiences; and craft evaluations that meet their needs rather than serve our agendas. Such an approach builds our clients' trust in us and enables us to nurture a long-lasting relationship that is mutually beneficial. In sum, in order for an evaluator-client relationship to evolve into a partnership, complementary needs and assets as well as compatible goals must be present, and trust should be nurtured.

Case Example. A couple of years ago we were hired by a local foundation to conduct an evaluation of a program providing direct assistance (for example, rent, utility, car, and medical bill payments; purchase of furniture and appliances; provision of food and clothing vouchers) to working-poor families and individuals in Los Angeles. The foundation initiated the evaluation to learn more about the effectiveness of the program, its strengths and weaknesses, and recommendations on how they could improve their internal evaluation processes. Our collective goal for the evaluation was to provide useful, actionable information that could be used for decision making. We approached the beginning of our relationship with the foundation much as we approach our other client relationships: building rapport, asking questions, and listening. We valued our clients' contribution to the evaluation and treated them as experts: they knew more than we did about their program and its stakeholders.

Once the partnership was initiated, we continued to nurture trust throughout the evaluation process. We worked closely with foundation staff to develop data collection instruments that would provide them with the information they wanted. We met with the foundation's advisory board for the program and with the board of directors to provide them information about the evaluation. As part of the program, the foundation partnered with nine community-based organizations; we relied on foundation staff to broker relationships with community partners rather than directly approaching them in our role as external evaluator. The evaluation went smoothly because we included the foundation staff in the evaluation activities and respected their contribution to the evaluation. They learned to trust us because we viewed them as content experts, communicated openly about evaluation activities, included them throughout the process, and listened closely to their concerns and needs. Since the completion of that initial report, our relationship with the foundation has endured and evolved. They continue to seek our advice on how to improve program activities, keep us updated on changes to the program, and invite us to key meetings and events. We are viewed by the foundation as integral to program improvement; we view our relationship with the foundation as one of our strongest and most promising partnerships.

NEW DIRECTIONS FOR EVALUATION • DOI: 10.1002/ev

Operations. In the operations stage, the real work of developing a partnership occurs: boundaries are negotiated, structures for decision making emerge, strategies for communication and information flow are developed, and other stakeholders become involved. A partnership between two or more individual organizations in essence becomes an organization itself during the operations phase, with members of each partner organization striving to improve the organizational performance of the partnership and meet specific goals. Like any other organization, a partnership requires effective internal structures and processes to ensure smooth governance, open communication, and accountability, as well as strong leadership (Waddock, 1989; Wohlstetter, Smith, and Malloy, 2005).

Governance and Communication. Explicit decision-making processes and governance structures are essential to effective partnerships. Such processes provide forums for stakeholders to come together, make decisions, and carry out the work of the partnership (Kanter, 1994; Waddock, 1989). In order for effective decision making to take place, it is essential to provide timely and appropriate information to all stakeholders. Partnerships must have open communication in which partners share the information needed to collaborate, including their objectives and goals, technical data, and challenges (Kanter, 1994).

In evaluator-client relationships, it is essential that the evaluator and the client establish guidelines and norms for decision-making processes and information flow. Open processes enable smooth governance and clear communication. Moreover, such processes help to sustain the trust and mutual respect that is necessary to sustain a long-lasting partnership. In our evaluations, we often create committees of invested stakeholders who can help us make better decisions about data collection processes or help us construct relevant data collection instruments. Regular meetings with key staff and stakeholders as well as consistent progress reports and e-mail updates from both the client and the evaluator ensure that the work of the evaluation is being carried out. We dedicate a large portion of our budget to decision making and communication processes because we view them as essential to developing effective client relationships.

Case Example. Approximately six years ago, we began working with a local professional school. We were initially hired to conduct a comprehensive review of the department and its curricular and degree programs. We began the process by inviting stakeholders within the professional school as well as representatives from key offices throughout the university (for example, provost's office, registrar) to serve on a committee that provided valuable feedback and helped us craft the evaluation. Such a forum encouraged the buy-in and cooperation we needed to conduct a successful evaluation, and it also helped us communicate more effectively with key stakeholders and make better decisions about evaluation activities, data collection processes, and reporting.

Accountability Plan. The operation of a partnership is most effective when an accountability plan guides the work of stakeholders. Das and Teng (1998) suggest that in order to facilitate effective operations in a partnership, the goals, structures, and processes for the partnerships must be clearly defined. An accountability plan establishes the outcomes for which each partner is responsible, outlines the constituents to whom the partner is accountable, and delineates the consequences of failure to meet established goals. In the field of evaluation, accountability plans often take the form of a letter of agreement, scope of work, memorandum of understanding, or contract. We have learned the importance of clearly specifying the responsibilities—what will and will not be provided—of all parties involved. Some of our most difficult relationships have been those in which roles and responsibilities have been unclear or attempts are made to modify the accountability plan without mutual consent after it has been established.

Moreover, we have also learned the importance of adhering to the guidelines established in our accountability plan in order to nurture mutual respect and maintain boundaries.

Case Example. A few years ago we began working with a community-based organization that provided after-school programs for at-risk youth. The organization received a grant to develop a new program focused on healthy eating and exercise and was required to evaluate the program by its funding agency. The budget was extremely limited for the evaluation; hence, we tried to be as specific as possible about our roles and responsibilities, most of which involved pre- and posttesting of students' knowledge about healthy eating and exercise. However, in the early stages of the project, the executive director frequently called on us to go beyond the scope of work and asked us to do searches for curriculum, review curricular programs and create lessons, and translate curriculum into multiple languages. We were invited to numerous staff and operational meetings in which the executive director would attempt to delegate additional tasks to us. We struggled initially to set boundaries and hold the client accountable for their roles and responsibilities. Over time, frustration with the client emerged, and the relationship ultimately suffered.

Leadership. Finally, effective leadership is necessary to manage the operation of a partnership and ensure that the work is carried out as intended. Effective leaders in collaborative relationships have three main roles (Smith and Wohlstetter, 2001; Wohlstetter, Smith, and Malloy, 2005):

- Architects, who are responsible for the day-to-day management of a partnership and create the internal structures and processes that enable key players to carry out the tasks at hand
- Information brokers, who distribute information throughout the partnership, ensuring that stakeholders have what they need to participate effectively

- Boundary spanners, who serve as liaisons to the external environment, providing other constituents with information about the partnership as well as buffering the partnership from unnecessary external noise

In evaluation partnerships, architects are often the project managers responsible for overseeing the evaluation process. They tend to be involved in the key decisions and monitor the day-to-day work of the evaluation. Both the client and the evaluator often serve as information brokers. The evaluator needs to communicate regularly about evaluation progress as well as provide evaluation reports that are actionable and easily understood. The client offers critical information about the evaluation to stakeholders who will serve as data sources and other constituents to enhance buy-in for both the evaluation process and results. Clients also often serve as the boundary spanner; they provide access to external data sources and broker relationships on behalf of the evaluator. In addition, they serve as the liaisons to external groups such as the media and funding agencies.

Personnel transitions often provide substantial challenges to partnerships and evaluations during the operations phase. When key leaders turn over, partners often have to reestablish the procedures and structures that guide the work of the evaluation. It may be more difficult to obtain access to data sources or disseminate essential information. Furthermore, potential changes to the organization or a specific program can affect the scope of work or evaluation design.

Case Example. We once worked with a foundation that provided social services to severely disabled low-income youth. The foundation received a grant to enhance its case management services, and the funding agency required an external evaluator. Our relationship with the agency began well, but soon suffered after the director of the grant left the foundation to pursue another position. Within a few months, the foundation had hired and lost two more grant directors. With each new director, we started again: we worked to build trust, create new communication structures, and establish leadership roles. We struggled to gain the information we needed to begin the evaluation; moreover, we had no liaison to broker relationships with stakeholders.

Evaluation. During the evaluation phase, the full range of impacts, both positive and negative, of the partnership is reviewed. The evaluation process provides partners with opportunities to identify areas for improvement and future directions. Modification of a partnership through a feedback loop commonly occurs after a partnership's impacts have been evaluated. This refinement often involves revisiting the operations phase to improve the structures and processes there or the initiation phase to redefine the goals of the partnership. In some cases, the evaluation phase results in the termination of a partnership. Termination does not necessarily indicate failure of a partnership; rather, the partnership may simply run its course and serve no future purpose (Waddock, 1989; Wohlstetter, Smith, and Malloy, 2005). In her study of business alliances, Kanter (1994) suggests several reasons for termination:

- A current partner may no longer be suitable because of new goals or a shift in direction.
- Personnel responsible for managing the relationship may be reassigned.
- New market conditions may render a partner unnecessary or unavailable.

Applied to the evaluator-client relationship, the evaluation phase often involves a reflection on the evaluation process, the quality of data obtained, and the accuracy of results. The client must determine whether the evaluation relationship yielded a successful evaluation product that can be used for the purpose intended. The evaluator must determine whether the evaluation process was satisfying and yielded the financial and professional benefits that were expected. Termination of an evaluation partnership can occur for several reasons: the client or the evaluator may find that the relationship was not beneficial, the client may need additional services that cannot be provided by the evaluator, or funding for evaluation services may become unavailable. Many of our partnerships are built on personal connections, and as a result, some of our partnerships have ended when critical leaders have been reassigned or have moved on to new positions.

Case Examples. At times, the evaluation phase may occur prior to the completion of the evaluation project. For example, we were hired to evaluate a program designed to provide natural environment assessments and case management services for young children. During the first reporting period, an analysis of output data revealed that limited case management services and assessments were being provided. Such a finding is typical of a start-up program, so we had little reason to be alarmed. During the second reporting period, there were few increases in outputs. We attempted to discuss our findings with the executive director but received no response or explanation. After a few months, we eventually terminated the relationship because we believed that the grant funding was not being used to provide the services intended by the funding agency. We subsequently learned that the organization had misappropriated funds from another grant to finance the construction of a new building.

In other instances, the evaluation phase can provide opportunities to expand on a promising relationship.

Case Example. Our partnership with the professional school mentioned earlier has grown considerably in the past six years. Every year since that initial project, we meet with the dean of the school to discuss the impact of current work, additional information needs, problems that require solutions, and potential areas for evaluation. This brainstorming session is one in which we meet as partners to generate new directions and endeavors for our relationship that lead us back to the initiation phase. We are not simply called on as a subcontractor to collect data when necessary; rather, we are viewed as a valuable external partner that is invested in the school's improvement. Our work with the professional school continues to grow; in fact, we are currently revisiting the initiation phase to work on developing a joint venture with the school.

Conclusion

Drawing on the literature base and our experiences in the field, we offer seven recommendations for nurturing effective client partnerships:

- Remember that your client also brings resources and expertise to the evaluation partnership.
- Work with clients who have compatible goals, and view evaluation as essential.
- Communicate openly, and listen to clients.
- Establish explicit decision-making processes and communication structures.
- Create and adhere to an accountability plan.
- Ensure that leadership is present and available.
- Evaluate your partnerships regularly, and modify them as necessary.

A successful evaluation endeavor requires the collaboration of the client, the evaluator, and other key constituents. In our experience, this collaboration is most likely to occur when the evaluator approaches the evaluator-client relationship as a partnership. Such an approach can build trust in the evaluation process, lead to actionable evaluation findings, and result in a mutually satisfying experience for both the client and evaluator.

References

Austin, J. E. *The Collaboration Challenge*. San Francisco: Jossey-Bass, 2000.

Bardach, E. *Getting Agencies to Work Together: The Practice and Theory of Managerial Craftsmanship*. Washington, D.C.: Brookings Institution Press, 1998.

Child, J., and Faulkner, D. *Strategies of Cooperation: Managing Alliances, Networks, and Joint Ventures*. New York: Oxford University Press, 1998.

Coe, B. A. "Open Focus: Implementing Projects in Multi-Organizational Settings." *International Journal of Public Administration*, 1988, 11(4), 503–526.

Das, T. K., and Teng, B. S. "Between Trust and Control: Developing Confidence in Partner Cooperation in Alliances." *Academy of Management Review*, 1998, 23(3), 491–512.

Dunn, J. A., Jr. "Transportation: Policy-Level Partnerships and Project-Based Partnerships." In P. V. Rosenau (ed.), *Public-Private Policy Partnerships*. Cambridge, Mass.: MIT Press, 2000.

Gray, B. *Collaborating: Finding Common Ground for Multi-Party Problems*. San Francisco: Jossey-Bass, 1989.

Gulati, R. "Social Structure and Alliance Formation Patterns: A Longitudinal Analysis." *Administrative Science Quarterly*, 1995, 40, 619–652.

Kamieniecki, S., Shafie, D., and Silvers, J. "Forming Partnerships in Environmental Policy: The Business of Emissions Trading in Clean Air Management." In P. V. Rosenau (ed.), *Public-Private Policy Partnerships.* Cambridge, Mass.: MIT Press, 2000.

Kanter, R. M. "Collaborative Advantage: The Art of Alliances." *Harvard Business Review,* July-Aug. 1994, pp. 96–108.

Oliver, C. "Determinants of Interorganizational Relationships: Integration and Future Directions." *Academy of Management Review,* 1990, *15*(2), 241–265.

Powell, W. W. "Neither Market nor Hierarchy: Network Forms of Organization." *Research in Organizational Behavior,* 1990, *12,* 295–336.

Ring, P. S., and Ven, A.H.V.D. "Developmental Processes of Cooperative Interorganizational Relationships." *Academy of Management Review,* 1994, *19*(1), 90–118.

Robertson, P. J. "Interorganizational Relationships: Key Issues for Integrated Services." In J. McCroskey and S. D. Einbinder (eds.), *Universities and Communities: Remaking Professional and Interprofessional Education for the Next Century.* Westport, Conn.: Praeger, 1998.

Rom, M. C. "From Welfare State to Opportunity, Inc.: Public-Private Partnerships in Welfare Reform." In P. V. Rosenau (ed.), *Public-Private Policy Partnerships.* Cambridge, Mass.: MIT Press, 2000.

Rosenau, P. V. "The Strengths and Weaknesses of Public-Private Policy Partnerships." In P. V. Rosenau (ed.), *Public-Private Policy Partnerships.* Cambridge, Mass.: MIT Press, 2000.

Schneider, A. L. "Public-Private Partnerships in the U.S. Prison System." In P. V. Rosenau (ed.), *Public-Private Policy Partnerships.* Cambridge, Mass.: MIT Press, 2000.

Smith, A. K., and Wohlstetter, P. "Reform Through School Networks: A New Kind of Authority and Accountability." *Educational Policy,* 2001, *15*(4), 499–519.

Sparer, M. S. "Myths and Misunderstandings: Health Policy, the Devolution Revolution, and the Push for Privatization." In P. V. Rosenau (ed.), *Public-Private Policy Partnerships.* Cambridge, Mass.: MIT Press, 2000.

Spillett, R. "Strategies for Win-Win Alliances." In F. Hesselbein, M. Goldsmith, and I. Somerville (eds.), *Leading Beyond the Walls.* San Francisco: Jossey-Bass, 1999.

Waddock, S. A. "Understanding Social Partnerships: An Evolutionary Model of Partnership Organizations." *Administration and Society,* 1989, *21*(1), 78–100.

Waide, P. J., Jr. "Principles of Effective Collaboration." In F. Hesselbein, M. Goldsmith, and I. Somerville (eds.), *Leading Beyond the Walls.* San Francisco: Jossey-Bass, 1999.

Weiss, J. A. "Pathways to Cooperation Among Public Agencies." *Journal of Policy Analysis and Management,* 1987, *7,* 94–117.

Wohlstetter, P., Malloy, C. L., Smith, J., and Hentschke, G. "Improving Service Delivery in Education: The Role of Cross-Sectoral Alliances." *Social Science Quarterly,* 2004a, *85*(5), 1078–1096.

Wohlstetter, P., Malloy, C. L., Smith, J., and Hentschke, G. "Incentives for Charter Schools: Building School Capacity Through Cross-Sectoral Alliances." *Educational Administration Quarterly,* 2004b, *40*(3), 321–365.

Wohlstetter, P., Smith, J., and Malloy, C. L. "Strategic Alliances in Action: Toward a Theory of Evolution." *Policy Studies Journal,* 2005, *33*(3), 419–442.

COURTNEY L. MALLOY *is a senior project manager with Vital Research, an independent consulting firm in Los Angeles.*

PATRICIA A. YEE *is a senior project manager with Vital Research, an independent consulting firm in Los Angeles.*

9

This chapter's case highlights the benefits new lines of business can provide for independent consulting firms and discusses the issues to consider and caveats.

Developing New Lines of Business: A Case Study

Judith Clegg, Dawn Hanson Smart

Developing a new line of business in an independent consulting firm provides an excellent way to expand, increase income for the company, and create cross-marketing opportunities. If it is not done correctly, however, this potential opportunity can imperil the existence of the business. This chapter describes how we mastered this challenge and what we learned along the way.

History

Initially, our firm's primary line of business focused on the provision of strategic planning for nonprofits and governments. We also conducted evaluations—mostly small efforts that examined whether social service programs were achieving the results they proposed in their funding applications. During the course of this work, we realized that very few nonprofit service providers, and perhaps even fewer funders, really understood what a client-focused outcome looked like. Nonetheless, many grant makers had begun asking their contractors to provide outcome data as part of contractual reporting.

In 1994 we decided to respond to the nonprofit agencies' requirement to measure outcomes and funders' need to better understand how to interpret the information they were requesting. We took a capacity-building approach, realizing that most nonprofits could not afford to hire a professional evaluator. Our goal was to teach our clients how to use program

NEW DIRECTIONS FOR EVALUATION, no. 111, Fall 2006   © Wiley Periodicals, Inc.
Published online in Wiley InterScience (www.interscience.wiley.com) • DOI: 10.1002/ev.199

theory to design more effective interventions and how to use sound evaluation methods to measure their results.

In order to pursue this venture, we partnered with another local consulting firm and created a collaborative venture. We articulated our mission as follows: to help organizations define and measure outcomes. Working collaboratively, we developed an array of training modules, publications, and coaching products for nonprofits and their funders. All of these products were user friendly and translated the complex concepts and language of outcome evaluation into materials that nonprofits, governments, and private grant makers could use to improve their expertise in program design and outcome measurement.

Following a year of product development, our collaboration was ready to roll out its products and services. Not surprisingly, we made a few mistakes in our initial marketing of the products. With a few course corrections, our workshop curricula, publications, and technical assistance tools have provided a steady stream of work for both of our firms for more than ten years. In addition, they have generated new evaluation clients, contracts, and opportunities.

Developing Products to Respond to the Market

Our initial offering was a full-day workshop covering foundational information on outcome measurement and the basics of evaluation design and planning. It included didactic and interactive activities around the following topics:

- Definitions and framework for outcome-based measurement
- Creating logic models
- Identifying outcomes
- Selecting indicators
- Evaluation design
- Data collection methods
- Procedures for evaluation planning and implementation

In the sessions, participants worked on their own programs and materials and left with a draft logic model and evaluation plan for a program. The manual we published served as the primary training material. A more in-depth publication provided detailed information on design and planning and was available for an additional fee. Content for the publications drew heavily on established evaluation texts such as Rossi and Freeman (1989) and Herman (1987).

Over the years, we customized the workshop to address clients' particular needs, expanding or contracting content elements and adding a coaching segment that provided feedback on participants' first efforts to create a logic model and evaluation plan. In time, we developed additional workshops to provide more technical training (surveying, focus groups, observation, record review, and data analysis) or more management-oriented sessions (managing change, links to strategic planning, and work process improvement), each with accompanying training workbooks.

Nonprofit organizations were the audience for these workshops, although grant makers sponsoring the sessions often participated as well. We came to recognize the importance of this as the work began to take shape: some funders contracted for multiple training sessions and accompanying technical assistance or coaching for the nonprofits, but many contracted for the training alone. It became clear that without additional support, many nonprofits were unable to make consistent progress in their evaluations, running into the inevitable roadblocks or problems inherent in evaluation. Grant makers whose staff had participated in the workshops were better able to provide assistance and coaching to their grantees than those who did not take advantage of the training opportunity.

We also realized that grant makers needed assistance to incorporate outcome information into their planning and decision making. The collaboration created content and materials specifically for grant maker staff and their board volunteers. These sessions were less formally structured, given the variability of different grant makers' approaches and systems for planning and allocations. In general, however, they focused on introductory information on logic models, outcomes, and indicators and allowed participants to practice reviewing agency materials, assessing agency proposals for alignment with organizational priorities, and using agency information in simulated allocation decisions. These sessions helped ensure that grant makers reviewing agency materials understood and had realistic expectations for their grantees' outcome measurement efforts. Other types of consultation for grant makers included work on their own outcomes, aligning organizational outcomes with community goals, developing and evaluating collaborative or community-based efforts, and other organizational issues related to outcome-based grants management.

Our Marketing Approach: Learning from Our Mistakes

We initially marketed directly to nonprofit organizations. Using traditional training recruitment techniques, we organized and advertised come-one-come-all sessions. We found that nonprofit organizations were interested but perceived our trainings as too expensive. As a consequence, turnout was poor. This initial lack of understanding of our market resulted in an expenditure of resources that we could not recoup. Learning from this experience, we shifted our marketing efforts to grant makers to convince them of the importance of training their grantees in outcome measurement. These subsequent efforts targeting grant makers as the primary client were more successful.

NEW DIRECTIONS FOR EVALUATION • DOI: 10.1002/ev

By this point, United Way of America (UWA) launched its outcome measurement initiative, creating a manual and training workshop covering the same content as our outcome measurement training. This proved fortuitous for our venture as it raised awareness of the importance of outcome measurement among the many nonprofit organizations funded through the UWA system. In addition, two staff members from our collaboration became UWA trainers available to United Ways around the country.

This opportunity provided an important boost to our new line of business by raising our visibility nationally and providing a steady stream of customers for training and coaching and additional revenue from follow-on contracts. While United Ways initially formed the bulk of our clientele, local and state governments regularly requested training. Federal government departments have not proven to be a source of many contracts, most likely due to their reliance on national methods and tools. Foundations were perhaps the last grant-making group to come on board, but eventually they came to represent a considerable portion of the business.

Benefits

The primary benefit of establishing a new line of business was the identification of new markets for consultants' skills and expertise. These markets enabled us to bring in additional revenue, support an expanded staff, and generate increased profits. This was particularly important for a relatively small company like ours with somewhat limited topical and geographical markets. We were able to expand our markets topically (that is, into greater emphasis on evaluation and into training) and geographically into a national market. This diversification expanded our customer base and ultimately replaced revenues lost due to a downturn in our primary market, resulting in greater resilience and stability for the firm.

Expansion into new topical and geographical markets bought us new clients with current and future needs. Not all new lines of business will yield the same benefits in this regard. For example, a typical training session brought us into contact with twenty to twenty-five potential new clients. An additional twenty to forty clients per year requested our publications, creating another source of contact with nonprofits and funders interested in evaluation. Clearly, training and publications offer a connection to a future customer base, a small portion of which will become clients for the company, contracting for either evaluation projects or other types of work. The ability to use our collaboration as a conduit into our other, primary line of business—planning and evaluation—generated work we would not likely have obtained otherwise.

The time and energy we put into developing our training and publication products brought us to a new level of expertise that we could market as well. For example, the expanded skill base in training and curriculum development also resulted in access to new clients. In recent years, we have

NEW DIRECTIONS FOR EVALUATION • DOI: 10.1002/ev

undertaken a number of curriculum development and training initiatives have that built on our learning and expanded our business to new service arenas.

After twenty-five years in social service consulting, the collaboration also provided an outlet to apply what we had learned about program effectiveness, program design, theory, and implementation in a new way. It posed a new challenge for our staff: how to take a capacity-building approach and use our expertise and skills in teaching nonprofits about evaluation.

Caveats

Our first caveat is to build on the knowledge base in your firm. If your primary expertise is in social services planning and evaluation, is a cruise line a good idea as a second line of business? Obviously you have to know something about the work to develop the quality products that clients buy. Developing evaluation publications and conducting training for nonprofits and their funders was a logical extension of our primary line of business. A corollary to this caveat is that if you bring in new staff to provide the requisite expertise, be sure they are a good fit and can build a market quickly enough to make them a good investment.

Second, knowing the content is not enough. You have to be a savvy business owner and marketer to expand successfully into new fields or geographical markets. Give yourself the entrepreneur test: Do you like taking some risks? Can you live with uncertainty? Can you commit money from your profit line to new business development? Can you sell your company's place in the new market?

Next, avoid mission creep. We work exclusively in the nonprofit and public sectors and are committed to helping organizations in these areas serve their clients. For-profit organizations have sought our services, but we have not pursued them. From our perspective, moving into the for-profit market is not a good fit with our values and represents a distraction from our mission that could result in a loss of nonprofit and foundation clients.

Finally, know when to pull the plug. Some new lines of business will not pan out. Be clear up front how much of your revenue you are willing to invest in a new line of business. You may invest more in product development and marketing than you ultimately reap in additional profit. Do not let a seemingly brilliant new market idea undermine the financial stability of your company.

Conclusion

Establishing a new line of business is not for everyone, but it offers independent consultants a valuable and potentially lucrative opportunity for expansion. Like any other new venture, it requires a serious commitment of your time, money, and energy. The good news is that it can be interesting, intellectually stimulating, and a means to capture new clients and generate expanded revenue.

We found a new line of business that was a good fit for our firm. Clearly, writing for publication is not for everyone. It takes time and effort, which may not be available to all independent evaluation consultants. Stand-up training may not be a good choice for some evaluators. It takes a particular personality to do it well and enjoy it. Publishing challenges you to put your expertise about evaluation into words, and saying it aloud by explaining it to others through training often clarifies your own understanding.

The message in our story is not about publishing or training; it is about finding a line of business you care about and doing your homework to make it a successful addition to your consulting business. As long as you keep your eye on the impact on your company's bottom line, new business ventures can serve you well.

References

Herman, J. L. *Program Evaluation Kit.* (2nd ed.) Thousand Oaks, Calif.: Sage, 1987.

Rossi, P. H., and Freeman, H. E. *Evaluation: A Systematic Approach.* (4th ed.) Thousand Oaks, Calif.: Sage, 1989.

JUDITH CLEGG is president of Clegg & Associates in Seattle, Washington, and cofounder and principal in the Evaluation Forum.

DAWN HANSON SMART is a senior associate at Clegg & Associates in Seattle, Washington, and a trainer and coach for the Evaluation Forum.

NEW DIRECTIONS FOR EVALUATION • DOI: 10.1002/ev

10

This chapter's case describes an innovative and replicable evaluation capacity-building strategy that benefited both the evaluation client and the independent consultant.

Evaluation Learning Circles: A Sole Proprietor's Evaluation Capacity-Building Strategy

Carolyn Cohen

The formal distance between evaluator and client that once characterized independent evaluations has given way to new options in working relationships. "Evaluator roles today are described by such terms as *facilitator, problem solver, educator, coach,* and *critical friend*" (Caracelli, 2000, p. 102). Drawing lessons from business restructuring practices that emphasize learning organizations, teamwork, and collaboration (Osterman, 1999; Stewart, 1992), evaluators have broadened the scope of their interactions with clients. Exemplary practice now entails actively engaging not only clients but other stakeholders as well, often by linking some combination of organizational development and training with evaluation (Patton, 1997). The ensuing opportunities to work in close partnership with clients are particularly rewarding for independent consultants who are sole proprietors. Benefits include the opportunity to use limited evaluation resources more efficiently, new means for incorporating professional development into a scope of work, increased opportunities for collegiality, and the mutual generation of new ideas for serving clients.

 The following case study illustrates my experience as a sole proprietor taking on the collegial roles of both learning partner and coach, using an evaluation capacity-building strategy I called an evaluation learning circle (ELC). Facilitating the ELC was one of a variety of tasks I conducted as part of a multiyear client relationship. In this chapter, I first outline the

NEW DIRECTIONS FOR EVALUATION, no. 111, Fall 2006 © Wiley Periodicals, Inc.
Published online in Wiley InterScience (www.interscience.wiley.com) • DOI: 10.1002/ev.200

approach, then identify elements leading to its success, and finally discuss the professional benefits of this replicable practice for independent consultants, particularly sole proprietors.

Background of the Case

The ELC was originally developed for the Puget Sound Center for Teaching, Learning and Technology (PSCTLT), a nonprofit charged with promoting the use of technology in education. The small staff, primarily educators, was characterized by the high energy levels and a can-do attitude associated with technology-oriented start-up businesses. Program managers chose to fund evaluation generously, allocating close to 15 percent of total grant funds. I had served as a consultant to the organization since its early formation, originally providing strategic advice and later serving as an external evaluator on grant-funded projects. Facilitating the ELC became one of many consulting duties.

The ELC concept developed during the evaluation of PSCTLT's first grants. While creating an evaluation plan for a key project, the staff and I struggled to develop project goals and a logic model. In support of this goal definition effort, the project director (now executive director) initially offered to send me to two sessions on program theory led by Patricia Rogers at the Evaluators' Institute. Then, at my suggestion, she agreed to attend herself so the two of us could work together as a team. When we returned, she convened a small group of staff members to further the work we had started in the workshops. Based on the success of that meeting, I proposed facilitating ongoing study sessions, so staff could become better consumers of and partners in evaluation efforts. The project director readily agreed. She identified staff members to be part of the circle, took charge of convening sessions, and made a point of always attending the meetings herself. This support continued when she became executive director.

The ELC group gathered every two to three months for nearly two years, meeting at the PSCTLT office for ninety-minute sessions. The meetings were informal and collegial and regularly attended by seven to eight people, including the identified staff members and other external evaluators affiliated with the organization.

The Learning Circle Defined

An evaluation learning circle can be described as a shared study experience whose purpose is to support the development of the client's evaluation capacity. The concept draws from a historical tradition of study circles, an adult learning strategy meant to empower as well as educate (Riel, Rhoads, and Ellis, 2006). Based on principles of effective workplace learning, it combines study of theory with reflection on practice in the context of work-related experiences. The ELC was not intended as a series of training sessions, but rather as a

NEW DIRECTIONS FOR EVALUATION • DOI: 10.1002/ev

participatory experience achieved through evaluator-facilitated co-learning sessions. While the evaluators who attended the sessions were resident experts, it was important to model that all professionals are on a learning continuum. As an evaluation strategy, the ELC aimed to enhance the client's ability to conduct internal evaluation and better use external evaluation findings. As an evaluator business strategy, it not only helped build the client's overall evaluation capacity, it furthered my own ability to understand client needs and better serve the organization.

Moving Toward a Co-Learning Experience

I served as the ELC facilitator, taking responsibility for leadership roles including generating topic ideas, disseminating reading materials, bringing in items relevant to the topic such as books and journals, preparing handouts and discussion guides, and facilitating the sessions. One goal was to encourage members to increasingly become teachers as well as learners and to take on these tasks themselves. In the beginning, this highly accomplished group of professional educators was not comfortable with the idea that they could lead learning activities on evaluation. Several strategies proved successful in moving toward shared responsibility for the educational experience. All members were expected to do some advance preparation, at minimum reviewing a suggested reading on the topic. Prior to some sessions, I also contacted specific participants and asked them to prepare for and lead one part of the discussion.

ELC topics were selected based on their relevance to client needs and interests. Over the course of the nearly two-year period, we addressed nine themes:

* Evaluation design
* Logic models
* Observations tools
* Focus groups
* Qualitative data analysis
* Online surveys
* Appreciative inquiry
* Success case method
* Evaluation theories

In preparation for one discussion—the success case method learning circle described below—every member was asked to review a different topical article. As a result, each had different information to share with the group, so no one could demur from participating with the excuse of having nothing new to add to the discussion. Over time, members increasingly took responsibility for preparing and training each other. Now that my contractual work is completed, the client plans to continue holding the circles led by, and for, internal staff.

Example: Success Case Method Learning Circle

Several weeks ahead of time, I sent an e-mail to ELC participants with Web links or attachments to the articles, presentations, and book reviews listed below. Each participant was asked to choose one of the following resources to review and to let the others know which they had selected so that all materials were covered:

- EvalTalk archives posts relating to the success case method
- "The Success Case Method: A New Way to Look at Organizational Change," a PowerPoint presentation by Gail Barrington
- "Using the Success Case Impact Evaluation Method to Enhance Training Value and Impact," a conference paper by Robert Brinkerhoff and Dennis Dressler
- *The Success Case Method,* by Robert Brinkerhoff (2003)
- A review of Brinkerhoff's book in the *Harvard Education Exchange* (Tulloch, 2003/2004)

I also sent out the following discussion guide, asking participants to keep the questions in mind when reviewing their source:

> Here is a suggested structure for our discussion. Based on the readings, let's work together to answer these questions.
> 1. What is the Success Case Method (SCM)?
> 2. How does it work? (i.e., let's try to figure out all of the steps and protocols)
> 3. What, if anything, is new or different about the SCM approach?
> 4. When would it be appropriate to use it in an evaluation? What types of evaluation questions might it best answer?
> 5. How would you report findings from an SCM-based study?
> 6. What are some examples when you have used something like this?
> 7. What concerns would you have about using this method? When would you not use it?

A carefully facilitated session encouraged full member participation and guided the discussion to focus on how SCM might be used in examining PSCTLT's professional development training programs. Members brainstormed ideas and also raised many concerns and questions about use. Some weeks later, SCM was the topic of several EvalTalk posts, so at a subsequent ELC, I asked one member to review and summarize them. This reinforced the learning and furthered the discussion of potential uses of SCM within the organization. The SCM lesson benefited staff and evaluator alike. One week after the session, PSCTLT staff felt confident enough to incorporate

SCM strategies in their response to a request for proposal. I also benefited from this exercise; it deepened my understanding of SCM, a technique I had not used, and opened up ideas for new ways to work with the organization.

This exhibit was originally presented in the form of a handout at the session entitled "Evaluator and Client Perspectives on Evaluation Capacity Building." Joint CES/AEA Conference. Toronto, Ontario. October 2005.

Necessary Ingredients

At heart, the ELC is an evaluation capacity-building practice, and independent consultants replicating this concept will benefit from the insights expressed by King (2002): ". . . The evaluator must become a teacher who purposefully structures evaluation and related activities and continuing reflection on these over time. Building capacity requires that the evaluator is integrally connected to people's work and alert to the programs that are potential objects for inquiry. . . . Interpersonal skills and the ability to identify and frame organizational issues are essential" (p. 76). The skills and attributes King notes are critical in successfully facilitating an ELC. In her keynote address to the 2004 United Kingdom Evaluation Society annual meeting, Patricia Rogers provided a context for understanding the role of ELCs in various types of capital development—human, social and institutional—using a program theory framework (Rogers, 2004). Her comments as a discussant in an American Evaluation Association (AEA) presentation on the ELC and other evaluation capacity-building efforts also noted characteristics contributing to its success: engagement with the client over time, trust building, providing a scaffolding to learning, a staged approach, and offering a safe place to admit a lack of knowledge.

The following success strategies derive from the experience to date:

1. Assess organizational readiness. Strategies such as the ELC may be most appropriate for an organization motivated by its existing learning culture (Davidson, 2001).

2. Embed the experience in an existing evaluator-client relationship. The facilitator should have a close enough working relationship with the organization to be familiar with the full range and scope of the client's projects.

3. Align topic selection with the client's immediate needs. Salience and relevance are key. Topic selection should be based on whether connections can be made to the client's current practice or needs.

4. Teach strategies in context, and provide reflection. The combination of practice and reflection is critical to understanding practical application. Strategies should be taught in context, with hands-on practice if possible.

5. Break the learning into manageable pieces, and follow up on previous topics. As Preskill and Torres note, learning is "incremental and iterative" (2000, p. 30). A ninety-minute session every other month seemed to be right. Past lessons were informally reinforced in the interim, for example, by forwarding an EvalTalk post relevant to a past ELC topic with a short suggestion on how to use this in current work.

6. Make the relationship a partnership. The evaluator is the content expert and the facilitator. But it is the evaluator-facilitator's job to help everyone own the sessions through various strategies that encourage participation and shared leadership.

7. Keep the atmosphere informal. Participatory learning thrives on collegiality. ELC sessions felt like a brief retreat. Members savored the opportunity to transport from the crush of daily deadlines and details for an hour and half to look at their work from a new perspective. Even the busiest members were truly reluctant to miss sessions.

Intersection of ELC Purpose with Organizational Mission and Culture

The ELC concept developed under optimum circumstances, in great part because its purpose aligned with both the client's external goals and its organizational culture. By its mission, PSCTLT is a nonprofit dedicated to providing innovative educator professional development. In combination with its culture of supporting internal training, this provided an ideal setting to engage staff in learning about evaluation. The ELC became a hub for identifying and supporting a host of other evaluation capacity-building efforts such as sending staff to training sessions and developing extensive internal resources. Sessions also served as one vehicle for reporting back on those efforts and discussing how to connect them to ongoing work.

Originally formed to help staff better understand and use evaluation findings, the ELC purpose evolved in many directions. In combination with other evaluation capacity-building efforts, it enabled staff to take on selected tasks originally assigned to me and eventually to become internal evaluators of their own projects. Over time, the executive director developed an interest in training her staff as external evaluators in order to provide the organization with an additional revenue source, and the ELC contributed to that training experience. It is also possible that the organization would not have continued supporting the ELC for as long as it did without the latter incentive.

Benefits to Independent Evaluation Consultants

Positive outcomes and substantial benefits for the client are the first and necessary conditions when considering an ELC. In this case, facilitating the ELC also had a synergistic effect: it sharpened my skills so I became better at supporting capacity-building efforts and in turn was better able to serve

NEW DIRECTIONS FOR EVALUATION • DOI: 10.1002/ev

my client. In using this practice, the evaluation consultant may enjoy additional benefits as well.

While all professionals must be efficient multitaskers, the pressure is intensified for those managing their own businesses. Evaluation capacity-building efforts are appealing in part because they serve multiple purposes. While the circle was intrinsically useful on its own, the experience also fostered connections to the staff and organizational initiatives, leading to new ideas about ways we could work together. Another outcome was that ELC participants felt comfortable contacting me frequently to ask questions and advice about their evaluation work, and I often passed along resources that would be useful or relevant to them.

Sole proprietors can successfully add this teaching-coaching role to their consulting repertoire and be assured that evaluation capacity-building tactics are not just in the province of large organizations, think tanks, and research laboratories. In fact, since those who work for themselves make all of their own decisions about allocating their time, they may have more flexibility in determining the types of services they choose to offer clients. Importantly, the format of providing short sessions in alternate months is not only a good dose for a client; it is manageable for someone in a sole practice.

While advantages may accrue for independent evaluation consultants in any setting, some are potentially more significant for sole practitioners. Specifically, increased efficiency in the use of evaluation resources, new options for personal professional development, and opportunities for collegiality may be more significant to someone with his or her own practice or to an evaluator in a small firm than for those in larger institutional settings.

Increases Efficient Use of Evaluation Resources. Evaluators working on their own are challenged and stretched thin by having to do it all. In a one-person shop, the owner oversees and may even conduct every task, from evaluation design to data entry. One outcome of the ELC was that it prepared the organization's internal staff to take on evaluation-related tasks that did not need to be performed externally. The coaching that took place through the combination of the ELC and related capacity-building efforts contributed toward providing skills and, perhaps as important, confidence to take on these assignments. As a result, my time was freed to concentrate on evaluation tasks that needed to be conducted externally or by someone with more experience. The time and resources saved allowed evaluation work to be accomplished far beyond the allocated budget. In some cases, a client may have internal resources that the evaluator lacks, such as a sophisticated technology infrastructure and expertise. That was true in the case profiled here. The ELC and related capacity building played a role in the client's decision to invest in high-end survey software and develop proficiency in designing and managing complex online surveys, far beyond the scope of what I could offer.

Incorporates Professional Development into Work Scope. Independent consultants often lack the prerequisites of institutional affiliation: in-house opportunities to hear invited speakers, participate in brown bag lunch forums, and access special funds for attending conferences and trainings. Taking time and allocating funds for independent learning often falls by the wayside under the crush of contract deadlines and managing the business. Facilitating the ELC as part of a scope of work allows the sole proprietor to make time for learning and to educate oneself as part of the contracted work. The very act of preparing for sessions and the facilitation itself, especially in the experiential context of applying learning to the ongoing projects of a client organization, is highly rewarding. Facilitator and participant alike gain from high-quality adult education experiences. Each learning circle is an opportunity to review journals, EvalTalk posts, and the latest books.

Offers Collegial Opportunities. Sole proprietorship has many advantages; however, it can be a lonely business. Working in partnership with clients and engaging with professional organizations such as AEA and local affiliates fills a need for collegial professional environments. The ELC adds another venue for the sole proprietor to build a professional development community, although it may not be a lasting one. In the case profiled, the fact that the organization's other external evaluators joined in added another layer of value and depth. A colleague whom I brought in to assist me on PSCTLT assignments attended the sessions, and this shared experience enhanced our joint work. In addition, through the ELC, one of the organization's other external evaluators and I formed a working relationship and are currently partnering on an evaluation for a different organization.

Conclusion

The case presented here relied on a long-term commitment from both the organization and the evaluator. While each of the seven success lessons noted above was critical to the ELC's positive outcomes, the cornerstones were the first two, both reflecting preexisting conditions: (1) a strong relationship between the independent consultant and client and (2) the organization's learning culture.

Organizations find themselves at various stages along a continuum of readiness for evaluation capacity building. Furthermore, independent consultants may not have the time or resources to commit to such an intensive model. Given these two realities, how does the independent evaluation consultant decide when to suggest strategies such as an ELC? What might be possible variations for organizations or evaluators who are not ready for this kind of long-term relationship? Based on this experience, the ELC appears to be a model that sole proprietors, and independent consultants in general, might replicate or adapt to their unique situations, but there are cautions. Since in this case the ELC was nested in other capacity-building efforts, it is unclear how this concept works as a stand-alone strategy. It may be that variations such as a three-session ELC or focusing over time on just one topic may be more workable for some clients and independent consultants.

Also, this strategy is somewhat of a luxury and most likely not feasible for the shoestring evaluation.

In sum, adding ELCs to a repertoire of evaluation capacity-building tools appears to be a promising strategy. It has a synergistic effect of offering the client multiple benefits, many of which benefit the independent evaluator. Future work on the ELC model, some already in progress, should more fully address underlying theory for best practice of ELCs and how the ELC model can connect and support other evaluation capacity-building efforts.

References

Barrington, G. V. "The Success Case Method: A New Way to Look at Organizational Change." A PowerPoint presentation presented at the Canadian Evaluation Society conference, Saskatoon, Saskatchewan, Canada, May 19, 2004.

Brinkerhoff, R. O. *The Success Case Method. Find Out Quickly What's Working and What's Not.* San Francisco: Berrett-Koehler Publishers, 2003.

Brinkerhoff, R. O., and Dressler, D. E. American Society for Training and Development Conference and Exhibition. San Diego, California, 2003.

Caracelli, V. "Evaluation Use at the Threshold of the Twenty-First Century." In V. Caracelli and H. Preskill (eds.), *The Expanding Scope of Evaluation Use.* New Directions for Evaluation, no. 88. San Francisco: Jossey-Bass, 2000, pp. 99–111.

Davidson, J. "Mainstreaming Evaluation into an Organization's 'Learning Culture.'" Paper presented at Evaluation: Mainstreaming Evaluation. Annual Meeting of the American Evaluation Association. St. Louis, Missouri, 2001.

Evaltalk archives. Accessed May 2005 and July 2005.

Cohen, C. "Evaluator and Client Perspectives on Evaluation Capacity Building." Joint CES/AEA Conference. Toronto, Ontario. October 2005.

King, J. "Building the Evaluation Capacity of a School District." In D. W. Compton, M. Baizerman, and S. H. Stockdill (eds.), *The Art, Craft, and Science of Evaluation Capacity Building.* New Directions for Evaluation, no. 93. San Francisco: Jossey-Bass, 2002, pp. 63–80.

Osterman, P. *Securing Prosperity, the American Labor Market: How It Has Changed and What to Do About It.* Princeton, N.J.: Princeton University Press, 1999.

Patton, M. Q. *Utilization-Focused Evaluation: The New Century Text.* Thousand Oaks, Calif.: Sage, 1997.

Preskill, H., and Torres, R. "The Learning Dimension of Evaluation Use." In V. Caracelli and H. Preskill (eds.), *The Expanding Scope of Evaluation Use.* New Directions for Evaluation, no. 88. San Francisco: Jossey-Bass, 2000, pp. 25–37.

Riel, M., Rhoads, J., and Ellis, E. "Online Learning Circles and Peer Reviews in Graduate Education." In T. Roberts (ed.), *Self, Peer, and Group Assessment in E-Learning.* Hershey, Pa.: Information Science Publishing, 2006, p. 145.

Rogers, P. Keynote Address. "Leading Horses to Water: Challenges in Building Evaluation Capacity." United Kingdom Evaluation Society. Glasgow, Scotland, December 2004.

Stewart, T. "The Search for the Organization of Tomorrow." *Fortune,* 1992, 125(10), 92–99.

Tulloch, T. Book review of *The Success Case Method: Finding Out What Works. The Evaluation Exchange,* Winter 2003/2004, IX(4), 16.

CAROLYN COHEN is the owner of Cohen Research and Evaluation based in Seattle, Washington.

11

Systematically assessing the performance of evaluation professionals allows evaluators to "walk the talk." Using this client-based evaluation method can be a valuable process for informing practice.

Evaluating the Evaluator: Development, Field Testing, and Implications of a Client-Based Method for Assessing Evaluator Performance

Kathleen Dowell, Jean Haley, Jo Ann Doino-Ingersoll

Improved services and client satisfaction are key aspects of independent evaluation consultants' practices. For evaluators to deliver the highest-quality services possible, they should regularly monitor their performance as evaluators, as well as the satisfaction of their clients. The client feedback form (CFF) was developed to gather performance assessment and satisfaction feedback from evaluation clients. Focusing on both performance assessment and client satisfaction provides evaluators comprehensive feedback regarding their services that they can then use to identify strengths and weaknesses and make appropriate adjustments to their work. This chapter discusses the importance of performance assessment and client satisfaction in general and within the field of evaluation and reviews the development and field testing of the CFF. Implications and future directions for the CFF are also discussed.

Performance Assessment

When not applied to programs, the terms *performance assessment, performance evaluation,* and *performance appraisal* are most commonly used in business management settings. Applied to the business of evaluation, performance assessment techniques can be an important part of a comprehensive quality

NEW DIRECTIONS FOR EVALUATION, no. 111, Fall 2006   © Wiley Periodicals, Inc.
Published online in Wiley InterScience (www.interscience.wiley.com) • DOI: 10.1002/ev.201

assurance strategy. Performance assessment has been shown to be a valuable component of many businesses' efforts to evaluate the performance of employees critically. Any course or book on business management or business leadership will contain a section on evaluating the performance of employees. Straub (2000) identifies two components to any performance appraisal: "the criteria against which employees are measured (such as quality of performance, job knowledge, and job-related behavior) and a rating scale that shows the level that employees have achieved on each criterion . . ." (p. 113). Performance evaluation is "the formal system by which managers evaluate and rate the quality of subordinates' performance over a given period of time" (Wideman, 2002).

One method for conducting performance evaluations that has recently experienced a rise in popularity is known as 360-degree feedback. Lepsinger and Lucia (1997) define the process as ". . . collecting perceptions about a person's behavior and the impact of that behavior from the person's boss or bosses, direct reports, colleagues, fellow members of project teams, internal and external customers, and suppliers" (p. 6). While asking clients to assess the performance of evaluators clearly falls within the domain of performance evaluation as defined by Straub and Wideman, it is only one aspect of the 360-degree process. The major difference between business definitions of performance assessment and client-based evaluator assessment is that the evaluation client rather than a manager or supervisor provides the feedback. Adding the peer review process to client-based assessment strategies would get one closer, although the peer review process undertaken as part of an "evaluating the evaluator" project (see Chapter Twelve, this volume) has focused on the product of the evaluation, that is, the report, rather than on the behavior of the evaluator.

Client Satisfaction

While performance assessment is one critical piece of information needed for quality assurance purposes, so is knowing whether consumers are satisfied with the services for which they are paying. In many areas of business and industry, companies and organizations focus a great deal of attention on satisfying the consumers of their products or services. In the broadest sense of the term, *client satisfaction* has been defined as "a complex process balancing consumer expectations with perceptions of the quality of the service or product in question" (Newsome and Wright, 1999, p. 161). According to Zeithaml and Bitner (1996), there are three types of client expectations: (1) desired service, which is the level of service a client hopes to receive; (2) adequate service, which is the minimum tolerable level of performance; and (3) predicted service, which is the level of service a client expects he or she is likely to receive. The authors state that consumers are able to recognize that service performance can vary and that consumers' willingness to accept this variation affects their perception of how satisfied they may be with a product or service, a phenomenon they refer to as the "zone of tolerance."

For most services, the zone of tolerance falls somewhere between desired services and adequate services. It is only when services fall outside the range of desired and adequate services that clients begin to notice service performance. Finally, it is the outcome of a service (rather than the service process) that has the greatest impact on the zone of tolerance and how much leeway clients are willing to give service providers. For evaluators, this suggests that final evaluation products and the overall perception of the quality of the evaluation are key aspects of client satisfaction.

Other researchers suggest additional factors that affect client satisfaction. For example, social equity theory suggests that clients will measure their gains with those of other clients and with those of the service provider (Oliver and Swan, 1989). Clients will be satisfied if they believe that their gains, compared to the resources they put out, are positive and fair. Furthermore, some emotional factors, for example, joy, excitement, pride, anger, and guilt, play into satisfaction (Oliver, 1993).

The majority of research on consumer satisfaction has been conducted in the fields of marketing and health care (Baker, Zucker, and Gross, 1998; Haag-Granello, Granello, and Lee, 1999; Kapp and Propp, 2002; Newsome and Wright, 1999); however, the theories and processes guiding efforts to measure consumer satisfaction in those fields apply to measurement of client satisfaction in the field of program evaluation. Measuring the satisfaction of evaluation clients is important for several reasons: (1) client satisfaction can be used as a quality control mechanism for evaluators; (2) satisfying evaluation clients may help independent evaluators compete and succeed in a sometimes highly competitive field by resulting in repeat business or referrals to other potential clients; and (3) it is fundamentally important for evaluators to know that they are meeting the needs of their clients because evaluation services cannot be considered high quality unless the client is satisfied.

Development of the Client Feedback Form

To bring both performance assessment and client satisfaction to the forefront of the evaluation field, a group of independent evaluation consultants developed the CFF to provide a systematic method for evaluation clients to assess the performance of evaluation professionals. The idea for the CFF originated at the annual meeting of the American Evaluation Association (AEA) in St. Louis, Missouri, in November 2001. The original discussion focused on two primary purposes for the CFF: to develop a tool for helping the Independent Consulting Topical Interest Group (IC TIG) identify professional development needs among its members and to "walk the talk," that is, put our words into action and follow the same advice we give our clients:

using evaluation as a valuable process to provide us opportunities to collect data systematically to inform our practices.

Following the AEA meeting in St. Louis, a committee developed a proposal for a think tank on evaluating the evaluator at the next AEA conference. For the 2002 annual AEA conference in Washington, D.C., the committee prepared a draft instrument that allowed for collection of feedback from the client's perspective. At the 2002 think tank session, participants reviewed and offered suggestions for improving the draft client feedback instrument. Based on these comments, in early 2003 the committee finalized the first version of what became known as the CFF. The group spent the remainder of 2003 pilot-testing the CFF, and its results were presented at the 2003 AEA conference.

Overview of the CFF Tool

The CFF starts with a question asking the respondent about his or her level of involvement in the project in question. Respondents are provided with nine choices and can select all that apply from the following list:

1. Involved in selecting the evaluator
2. Provided input to the evaluation plan
3. Key decision maker (for example, approved instruments, reports, changes in the plan, and so on)
4. Day-to-day point of contact with the evaluator
5. Handled my organization's responsibilities in the evaluation
6. Approved invoices/interim status reports
7. Read/commented on final evaluation report/s
8. Participated in interpreting results/writing recommendations
9. Other

For the final option, respondents are asked to specify their response. This first question provides context for the responses that follow.

The respondent's role clarification is followed by ratings of overall quality and usefulness of the evaluation and whether the respondent would recommend the evaluator to colleagues. This last item is followed by an open-ended question asking the respondent to explain his or her response. These questions are designed primarily to assess evaluator performance.

The next item on the form presents the respondent with seven dimensions of evaluator performance, some of which are drawn from the Program Evaluation Standards, which were developed by the Joint Committee on Standards for Educational Evaluation (www.eval.org). These performance dimensions refer to the evaluator's:

1. Understanding of the project
2. Attentiveness to my needs/organization's needs

3. Quality of reports/products produced
4. Appropriateness of reports/products for my needs/organization's needs
5. Timeliness in delivering reports/products
6. Accessibility to me/my organizations
7. Communication with me/my organization

This question also gives the respondent the opportunity to add any other dimension of performance that was not included in the list. Respondents are asked to rate each item on a four-point scale: poor, fair, good, or excellent. If a particular dimension is not applicable to the project or if respondents are unsure of how to rate a particular item, they have the opportunity to select "NA/Don't Know." While the dimensions described in this question concern the evaluator's performance, clients are essentially providing their level of satisfaction with the evaluator's performance.

Directly after providing ratings on the dimensions of evaluator performance, respondents are asked to describe in their own words the strengths of the evaluator and areas where the evaluator could benefit from improvement. These questions provide more detailed information for evaluators to improve their services, as well as to identify areas where the evaluator should continue to operate in the same way as in the past. This series of questions allows the client to provide further opinions as to the evaluator's performance.

The final formal rating question on the CFF asks respondents to rate the evaluator's adherence to eight of the Twenty-Five Guiding Principles for Evaluators that AEA developed "to guide the professional practice of evaluators, and inform evaluation clients and the general public about the principles they can expect to be upheld by professional evaluators" (www.eval.org). The principles selected for the form were those that were most appropriate for evaluation clients to rate. Most principles not included in the CFF include items that the majority of clients would find difficult to assess, such as, "To ensure the accuracy and credibility of the evaluative information they produce, evaluators should adhere to the highest technical standards appropriate to the methods they use" (Guiding Principle A.1). While it is true that some clients will have the ability to respond to this guideline, many more would not. Respondents are given four choices for each of the above questions: (1) NA/don't know, (2) no, (3) partially, and (4) completely. As with most other instruments of this kind, the final question on the CFF reads, "Do you have any other comments about your experience working with the evaluator on this particular project? If yes, please feel free to use the space below."

Pilot Testing of the CFF

In early 2003, after development of the first draft of the CFF, the committee sent out a call to members of the IC TIG's electronic discussion group for volunteers to pilot-test the CFF. Twelve evaluators volunteered. Completed CFFs were collected from thirty-four clients who completed either hard copy or online versions of the form. Evaluators were not given direction regarding who should complete the CFF. It was left to the evaluators to determine who at their client agencies would be the most appropriate respondents. Evaluators were asked to collect the CFF forms from their clients and then submit the forms to a third party for data entry and analysis. Results for each individual evaluator were then sent back to the evaluator by e-mail. This approach reduced concerns about client confidentiality by having a third party enter and analyze the raw data, with evaluators receiving data files stripped of client identification.

Clients who completed the CFF during the pilot phase were highly involved with the evaluator-evaluation project they were asked about, with 100 percent reportedly providing input into the evaluation plan for the project, 91 percent considering themselves key decision makers about their project, 79 percent providing input into the selection of the evaluator for the project, and 74 percent considering themselves the day-to-day point of contact for the evaluator. These results suggest that evaluators were successful in identifying appropriate people at their client agencies to complete the CFF, and the clients who completed the form were qualified to address evaluator performance adequately and provide feedback on satisfaction because they were highly involved in the evaluation projects in question.

Table 11.1 displays results for CFF questions focusing on client satisfaction. As shown, 91 percent of clients rated the quality of the evaluators' work as excellent or very good, 91 percent rated the usefulness of the evaluators' work as extremely or very useful, 91 percent rated the quality of reports/products as excellent or good, 94 percent rated the appropriateness of reports/products as excellent or good, and 97 percent rated timeliness in delivering reports/products as excellent or good. In addition, 94 percent of clients said they would recommend the evaluator to their colleagues. Common reasons for recommending the evaluator to colleagues were knowledge and expertise in evaluation, having a pleasant/personable interaction style, thoroughness and attention to detail, and professionalism.

Key findings regarding performance assessment are set out in Table 11.2. As shown, 88 percent of clients rated the evaluators' understanding of the project as excellent or good; 97 percent rated attentiveness to clients' needs as excellent or good; 94 percent rated accessibility of evaluation staff as excellent or good; and 91 percent rated communication as excellent or good. Performance was also measured by asking clients to identify evaluators' strengths. The two most common strengths identified by clients were technical skills/analytical skills/data interpretation and writing/presentation skills. Each of these skills was identified as evaluator strengths by 28 percent of the respondents. Other strengths, each identified by 21 percent of clients, included understanding client needs, communication skills, and dedication/commitment/enthusiasm toward the evaluation project. Clients

Table 11.1. Client Satisfaction Pilot Test Results for CFF

Satisfaction Dimension	Response	Percentage
Overall assessment of the quality of the work	Excellent	85
	Very good	6
	Good	6
	Fair	3
	Poor	0
Usefulness of the work performed	Extremely useful	73
	Very useful	18
	Somewhat useful	9
	Not at all useful	0
Quality of reports/products	Excellent/good	91
	Fair/poor	9
Appropriateness of reports/products	Excellent/good	94
	Fair/poor	6
Timeliness in delivery of reports/products	Excellent/good	97
	Fair/poor	3
Would recommend evaluator to others	Yes	94
	No	6

Note: N = 34.

Table 11.2. Performance Assessment Pilot Test Results for CFF

Performance Assessment Dimension	Excellent/Good	Fair/Poor
Understanding of project	88%	12%
Attentiveness to client needs	97	3
Accessibility of evaluation staff	94	6
Communication	91	9

Note: N = 34.

identified a number of opportunities for evaluators to improve their work. The most common suggestion was for better report writing (40 percent), followed by deeper understanding of project (30 percent) and improved communication and interpersonal style (30 percent).

Responses to the questions regarding evaluator adherence to the AEA Guiding Principles indicated that most evaluators, from the clients' perspectives, effectively adhered to the guidelines. Table 11.3 displays the percentage of clients who reported that their evaluator completely adhered to specific Guiding Principles. The Guiding Principles with the largest percentages of clients reporting complete adherence were negotiating honestly with the organization (94 percent), conducting the evaluation in a way that

Table 11.3. Client Assessment of Evaluator Adherence to AEA Guiding Principles Pilot Test Results for CFF

Guiding Principle	NA/Don't Know	No	Partially	Completely
1. Did the evaluator negotiate honestly with your organization concerning:				
Costs?	6%	0%	0%	94%
Tasks to be undertaken?	3	0	3	94
Limitations of methods?	9	6	6	79
Scope of results likely to be obtained?	12	6	3	79
Uses of data resulting from the evaluation?	6	0	12	82
2. Did the evaluator explore with you/your staff both the shortcomings and strengths of various evaluation questions and the approaches . . . ?	9	0	18	73
3. Did the evaluator record all changes made in the original negotiated project plans and the reasons why the changes were made?	36	6	6	52
4. Did the evaluator conduct the evaluation in a way that clearly respects the dignity and self-worth of stakeholders?	6	0	3	91
5. Did the evaluator identify and respect differences among participants and consider the implications of such differences when planning . . . ?	15	0	12	73
6. Did the evaluator include the perspectives/interests of all stakeholders?	9	3	15	73
7. Did they communicate their methods/approaches accurately . . . ?	9	0	6	85
8. Re: reporting negative findings, did the evaluator seek to maximize the benefits and reduce any unnecessary harm that might occur . . . ?	32	0	15	53

Note: N = 34.

respects the dignity and self-worth of stakeholders (91 percent), and communicating methods and approaches accurately (85 percent).

These initial findings from the field test of version 1 of the CFF suggested that the CFF could successfully provide feedback from clients on key dimensions of both performance and client satisfaction. Findings also indicated that the CFF was successful in helping evaluators identify areas of professional strength and weakness. After the pilot test was completed, there was growing interest in finding out exactly how useful the evaluators who used the CFF thought the form was in helping them with their own quality assurance strategies. The primary questions were: (1) Did results of the CFF provide evaluators with information they could use to assess their performance and quality of work? and (2) Was the CFF a user-friendly tool that both evaluators and clients would consider using?

To address these questions, the twelve evaluators who participated in the CFF pilot test were surveyed regarding their experience using the CFF with their clients. Surveys were e-mailed to all evaluators who participated in the field test, and evaluators were asked to complete the survey and return the completed survey by e-mail. Of the twelve evaluators surveyed, 42 percent reported giving their clients the online version of the CFF, 25 percent gave their clients a hard copy to complete, and 33 percent offered their clients the choice of either the hard copy or online version. Of forty-nine clients asked to complete the CFF, thirty-four clients completed and returned the CFF, giving an overall response rate of 69 percent.

To determine if the CFF provided evaluators results they could use for quality assurance strategies, evaluators were asked a series of questions regarding their use of CFF results. One-third of the evaluators reported that they used the results of the feedback forms. Ways in which they used the results included:

- To better understand how clients used and rated their services
- To think about how to best approach and work with clients
- To identify and address negative comments made by clients
- To raise staff morale by sharing positive feedback from clients with the evaluation staff

Over half the evaluators reported not using the results of their CFFs. The most common reason for not using the results was that all the client comments were positive and did not provide the evaluator any ideas for changing his or her work approach. One evaluator reported never receiving CFF results from the third-party data manager, and another evaluator had concerns over client honesty and questioned the client's ability to understand the form, particularly the section on the AEA Guiding Principles. When asked how they would use the results in the future, evaluators reported that they:

- Intended to complete summary analyses to get an overall rating of services and to identify areas of weakness
- Would include CFF findings when creating marketing materials
- Would use the results to assess performance and make needed changes

Overall, 67 percent of the evaluators thought the CFF was a useful tool for assessing their performance. Evaluators reported that the CFF was useful in assessing performance because it highlighted aspects of their work that the clients valued, helped the evaluator know if he or she was on track with the client, provided evaluators with testimonials they could use for marketing purposes, and provided data that the evaluator could use to pinpoint areas of strength and weakness.

To address the question of whether the CFF was a user-friendly tool for the evaluators and clients, evaluators were asked about the barriers they encountered while using the form. They were also asked to identify ways in which the process could be improved. Evaluators identified a number of ways to improve the CFF process:

- Clarify who is to fill out the form, particularly if there is more than one person at the client agency with whom the evaluator deals.
- Ensure that evaluators receive their raw data files back in a timely manner.
- Make raw data files available to the evaluators in a format that is immediately usable.
- Create a version of the CFF that is appropriate for use while an evaluation is in progress (rather than having to wait until the end).
- Add questions about interactions between clients and the evaluators.
- Clarify what is to be assessed (that is, the overall evaluation versus specific individuals).

The pilot test identified a number of barriers to using the CFF. First, some evaluators were uncertain about how to introduce the form to their clients. This uncertainty stemmed mostly from being unsure about how to tell the clients what the form's purpose was and when to introduce it to the client. Other evaluators felt uncomfortable asking the client to complete the form because they knew their clients were extremely busy. A second barrier dealt with timing: knowing the best time in the life of a project to ask a client to complete the form. For example, some evaluators questioned whether the form should be used only when a project was finished or whether the form could be used at other times as well. Some of the questions were geared specifically to end-of-project timing, so introducing the form at other times was not appropriate. As a result of this difficulty, several evaluators expressed an interest in having a form that could be used at various times during the life of a project. Third, some evaluators reported client resistance to completing the CFF, either because the client was too busy (that is, clients view the CFF as "one more thing to do") or because they simply were not interested in completing the form.

Another barrier was related to entry and analysis of CFF data. During the pilot phase of the CFF, evaluators were not required to enter their own data into a database for analysis. After the initial pilot phase, however, evaluators were told that data entry would no longer be handled by a third party and that evaluators themselves would be required to do their own data entry. Several evaluators then expressed resistance to entering and analyzing their CFF data, mostly because they were too busy and CFF data entry was seen as "one more thing to do." Fifth, evaluators reported client concerns that clients' responses would not be anonymous (that is, "the evaluator will know who I am"). Finally, some evaluators reported that the form was not suitable for the type of work they were conducting. Personnel or product assessments were examples of work that evaluators felt did not fit well with the types of questions included on the CFF.

Following the initial pilot testing of the CFF, several iterations of the tool were developed. Feedback from evaluators at the 2003 AEA meeting suggested that the section of the CFF that included the Guiding Principles may be difficult for clients to complete. Furthermore, they suggested that clients would more readily accept a shorter form (one page front and back). Based on these comments, two versions of the CFF emerged: the original CFF, which contains a series of question regarding evaluators' adherence to the Guiding Principles, and a shortened version in which the questions about the Guiding Principles are omitted.

In addition to wanting a shortened version of the CFF, several evaluators expressed concern that the language used in the Guiding Principles section of the long form was confusing. Therefore, that section was reworked so that the language used more common terms. The final version of the Guiding Principles section includes the following questions:

1. Did the evaluator negotiate honestly with your organization concerning:
   - Costs?
   - Tasks to be undertaken?
   - Limitations of methods?
   - Scope of results likely to be obtained?
   - Uses of data resulting from the evaluation?
2. Did the evaluator explore with your staff both the shortcomings and the strengths of different ways to evaluate your program?
3. Did the evaluator record all changes made in the original evaluation plan and the reasons why the changes were made?
4. Did the evaluator conduct the evaluation in a way that clearly respects the dignity and self-worth of everyone involved?
5. Did the evaluator identify and respect differences among participants (for example, age; gender; ethnicity; etc.) when planning, conducting and reporting the evaluation?
6. In planning and reporting the evaluation, did the evaluator consider including the perspectives and interests of all interested parties?
7. When the evaluator presented his or her work, did he or she communicate accurately and in sufficient detail to allow others to understand, interpret and critique it?
8. Did the evaluator report negative findings in a sensitive manner without compromising the integrity of the findings?

Further discussion at the 2003 AEA conference included the suggestion that the committee try to broaden the scope of use of the finalized versions of the CFF beyond the IC TIG. To accomplish this, the CFF committee approached AEA with the request to post both versions of the form on its Web site so that evaluators visiting the site could download and use copies of the instrument. AEA posted both versions of the CFF at http://eval.org/iccff.htm. A brief introduction to the forms is available on the site, along with the names and e-mail addresses of the form's developers.

While most members of AEA have received a specific request at some point during the project to use the form, AEA members and nonmembers alike have made specific requests to obtain and use the CFF. Since the inception of the project, there have been over thirty specific requests to use the form, including one Fortune 500 corporation, one U.S. school district, one U.S. state agency, one training organization, two U.S. federal agencies, two private U.S. foundations, two private nonprofit organizations (one U.S., one Australian), four universities (three U.S., one Australian), and nineteen independent consultants or independent consulting firms that span the United States and Canada. In addition to using the instrument for client satisfaction and performance evaluation, other uses cited in requests included using the form for a strategic development planning process, providing an informational handout for evaluation training, and providing a tool to grantees to use with their evaluators (foundations and public agencies).

Lessons Learned and Future Directions for the CFF

The development and use of the CFF has opened the eyes of many evaluators to the importance of asking evaluation clients to evaluate their work systematically on important dimensions of both client satisfaction and performance. The CFF is a user-friendly form that provides evaluators one means of gathering feedback on how well they are performing. A pilot test of the CFF demonstrated the value of the data that evaluation clients can obtain. Many evaluators who pilot-tested the CFF reported positive experiences with the form and the information it provided. Most important, evaluators reported being able to use the data to assess their overall performance and help pinpoint areas of their work where improvement may be needed. From a quality assurance perspective, these data can be invaluable as evaluators continually seek to improve their work.

The primary advantage of using the CFF is the ability to receive direct feedback on specific dimensions of an evaluator's work. All evaluators dedicated to professional growth and development can benefit from such feedback. When responses are positive, consultants can potentially use direct quotations and aggregate ratings over time (given respondents' express permission to do so) in marketing materials. On a larger scale, the tool could be helpful in identifying areas of professional development that are needed for a specific group of evaluators, such as the IC TIG of the AEA or even a local affiliate.

The process of developing the CFF has been a learning experience for all involved. Based on feedback from evaluators who used the form, the CFF should continue to evolve into a method of client feedback that becomes easier to use and provides more useful data to evaluators. Future CFF efforts may benefit from several changes or options that will allow for greater ease of use. For example, CFF use might be enhanced if clients are provided the certainty of remaining anonymous, that is, allowing them to send CFFs to a central location for data processing and analysis. For optimal functioning, the third-party data entry would provide evaluators with a raw data file that is ready for analysis, with no additional manipulation required. This approach would ease the burden of evaluators in using the form and may increase its use. However, this would require a much greater level of effort on the part of the project's sponsors than is currently possible.

During the pilot phase of the CFF, more clients submitted their feedback using the online version of the tool than hard copies. Offering clients and evaluators a permanent online version of the CFF tool may also increase use of the CFF. Ideally, an online version would allow clients to have remote access to the form and submit results in a completely anonymous manner. This approach would solve two problems associated with the CFF. First, it would reduce client and evaluator concerns about the confidentiality of client data, thus increasing the likelihood that clients will provide candid and truthful feedback. Second, the online form may make the logistics of the CFF process easier, as the evaluator will simply have to provide the client with the URL of the online form in lieu of preparing hard copies of the form that need to be mailed to clients. While an online approach seems to address some concerns, the costs of a Web-based instrument could impede this possibility.

Finally, it has been suggested that it would be beneficial for the profession if AEA took on the task of monitoring members' client satisfaction. A process proposed during an electronic discussion of the form included having evaluators build into their contracts with clients the completion of the form at the end of the project. To maintain client anonymity, forms would be returned to AEA, where they would be coded for analysis. After three forms have been submitted for any one evaluator or firm, an aggregate report would be sent to the evaluator. To help defray the cost of administering this effort, evaluators could either pay an annual fee or pay a fee per CFF sent out and completed. Such a program would benefit individual evaluators and firms, as well as the profession as a whole. As one TIG member noted, an approach such as this would put evaluators one step ahead of any other profession, which would be appropriate since the CFF is, in essence, an evaluation process and AEA is an evaluation association.

Conclusion

In the same way that clients' customers and project participants are excellent sources of information regarding the quality, importance, and usefulness of clients' programs, clients are excellent sources of information on the quality, importance, and usefulness of evaluators' products and services. The CFF offers evaluators one possible method for obtaining client feedback. However, it should be noted that the CFF is not offered as a comprehensive method for assessing evaluator performance; just as clients cannot rely solely on program participants to evaluate their programs, evaluators cannot rely solely on clients to evaluate their performance. For a fully comprehensive look at evaluator performance, other aspects of the project must be reviewed. For example, without looking at how a project was designed and the processes used for project implementation, feedback from clients cannot reveal much about why the quality or usefulness of a project was rated high or low. In the case of evaluating the evaluator, the job of examining the design and methods for collecting and analyzing data must be that of our colleagues who are far more qualified to perform the task. Nonetheless, clients are valuable sources of information regarding certain aspects of evaluators' work. As more evaluators become aware of the CFF, the CFF may become an integral part of many evaluators' quality assurance strategies.

References

American Evaluation Association. "Guiding Principles for Evaluators." *American Journal of Evaluation,* March 2006, *27,* 5–6.

Baker, L., Zucker, P., and Gross, M. "Using Client Satisfaction Surveys to Evaluate and Improve Services in Locked and Unlocked Adult Inpatient Facilities." *Journal of Behavioral Health Services and Research,* 1998, *25,* 1113–1129.

Haag-Granello, D., Granello, P., and Lee, F. "Measuring Treatment Outcomes and Client Satisfaction in a Partial Hospitalization Program." *Journal of Behavioral Health Services and Research,* 1999, *26,* 1094–1112.

Kapp, S., and Propp, J. "Client Satisfaction Methods: Input from Parents with Children in Foster Care." *Child and Adolescent Social Work Journal,* 2002, *19,* 227–245.

Lepsinger, R., and Lucia, A. D. *The Art and Science of 360 Degree Feedback.* San Francisco: Jossey-Bass/Pfeiffer, 1997.

Newsome, P., and Wright, G. "A Review of Patient Satisfaction: 1. Concepts of Satisfaction." *British Dental Journal,* 1999, *186,* 161–165.

Oliver, R. "Cognitive, Affective, and Attribute Bases of the Satisfaction Response." *Journal of Consumer Research,* 1993, *20,* 418–430.

Oliver, R., and Swan, J. "Equity and Disconfirmation Perceptions as Influences on Merchant and Product Satisfaction." *Journal of Consumer Research,* 1989, *16,* 372–383.

Straub, J. *The Rookie Manager.* New York: AMACOM, 2000.

Wideman, M. *Wideman Comparative Glossary of Common Project Management Terms,* v. 3.1. 2002. http://www.maxwideman.com/pmglossary/PMG_P01.htm. Accessed May 16, 2006.

Zeithaml, V., and Bitner, M. *Service Marketing.* New York: McGraw-Hill, 1996.

KATHLEEN DOWELL *is a partner with Partners in Evaluation and Planning, an independent evaluation and program planning consulting firm in Sykesville, Maryland.*

JEAN HALEY *is president of Haley Consulting Services, a private consulting firm located in Chicago, Illinois.*

JO ANN DOINO-INGERSOLL (1956–2006) *was president of Strategic Research, an education and human services consulting firm in Mahwah, New Jersey.*

This chapter describes a peer review model for facilitating professional growth developed within the context of the American Evaluation Association's Independent Consulting Topical Interest Group.

12

Nurturing Professional Growth: A Peer Review Model for Independent Evaluators

Sally L. Bond, Marilyn L. Ray

There has been a recent groundswell of support in the American Evaluation Association's Independent Consulting Topical Interest Group (IC TIG) for evaluating evaluators' work just as evaluators evaluate the work of their clients. To facilitate this self-evaluation, the IC TIG elected to create a peer review process that focuses on written evaluation products. Through participation in the resulting peer review model, evaluation colleagues engage in constructive and respectful critiques of their peers' evaluation reports. The process affirms strengths in written communication and identifies areas for growth. We are the principal architects and cochairs of the IC TIG Peer Review and in this chapter discuss the unique needs of independent evaluators for professional feedback and describe the model we have designed to work in the context of a community of independent evaluators. Other communities of independent evaluators may find this model or a variation of it useful for their own professional development.

Independent Evaluators and Professional Development Needs

Many evaluators work as consultants in solo or very small practices that afford few, if any, opportunities for feedback from colleagues on their practice and products. In formal organizations that conduct evaluations, colleagues often review each other's work and give feedback before it is

New Directions for Evaluation, no. 111, Fall 2006 © Wiley Periodicals, Inc.
Published online in Wiley InterScience (www.interscience.wiley.com) • DOI: 10.1002/ev.202

finalized for a client. Independent evaluators, who routinely work alone, are at a disadvantage in this regard. New professionals in the field, especially those who were not trained in graduate evaluation programs, may not be aware that high-quality evaluation reports routinely address the nature and context of the program, methods used to generate and analyze evaluation findings, and defensible conclusions drawn from systematic data analyses. Evaluators who enter the field after years of practice in a substantive area (for example, health, education or social services) are not necessarily familiar with the *AEA Guiding Principles for Evaluators* (2005) or with other evaluation standards documents, such as *The Program Evaluation Standards: How to Assess Evaluations of Educational Programs* (Joint Committee on Standards for Educational Evaluation, 1994).

No matter what substantive areas they work in or how they come to the field of evaluation, peer review is a viable strategy for helping professional evaluators understand and improve the quality of their written communication with clients. Review criteria in the IC TIG model focus on the most basic elements of a high-quality evaluation report: project description, evaluation methodology, findings, conclusion and recommendations, and overall quality of the writing and presentation. The peer reviewers' job is to analyze evaluation reports in the light of a framework of questions for each report element. For example, a question related to program description is, "Is the program—for example, its context, purposes, procedures, funding source, and program goal(s)—described sufficiently for the intended audience to understand what is being evaluated?" Reviewers' analyses of each report element are first summarized in written comments and then rated on a six-point scale ranging from "Not addressed" (0) to "Skillfully addressed" (5). Reviewers are instructed to provide specific examples in their comments, especially when discussing elements that were not adequately addressed. In the final "General Comments" section of the review, reviewers point out aspects of the report that were particularly helpful and offer suggestions for improvement of future reports.

A Model for Other Communities of Independent Evaluators

Peer reviews are used in a variety of contexts to maintain established standards of practice and foster professional growth. For example, peer review processes are used by schools to improve classroom teaching practices, by publishers and funding agencies to screen and select from submissions, and by doctors to assess the quality of work and compliance with accepted medical practices. In many contexts where peer review is practiced, participation is expected or required as a condition of employment, tied to a professional certification process, or necessary for professional validation and the receipt of tangible rewards, such as publication or a job promotion.

As in other contexts, independent evaluators have a set of standards to guide their work. These standards for the professional conduct of program evaluators are clearly stated in the *AEA Guiding Principles for Evaluators* (2004). Unlike many other peer review processes, however, the participation of independent evaluators is completely voluntary. There are no external incentives or requirements to motivate participation in the process, only the intrinsic desire to improve one's practice. By virtue of being independent evaluators, interactions among them are likely to be limited. Therefore, relatively few of them are likely to have ongoing working relationships with one another.

Working within the context of independent evaluation consulting requires designing a process that independent evaluators who are mostly unknown to each other will be comfortable engaging in and creating the expectation that participants will gain useful insights into the effectiveness of their written communication.

Comfort of Engagement. Both of us, long-time, active members of AEA's IC TIG, have tried several strategies to make other independent evaluators aware of and comfortable with the idea of participating in a peer review process. Since agreeing to initiate the process, we have presented our ideas and solicited feedback from other independent evaluators at IC TIG business meetings and annual reviewer orientation sessions. Every presentation has been used to emphasize that the peer review is an opportunity for professional growth, not a ploy to check up on the work of others. The peer review process is double-blind, in that the identities of reviewers and reviewees are known only to the cochairs. Reports are submitted to the cochairs for review and assigned to three available reviewers. Review guidelines, freely shared with anyone who is interested in participating, provide suggestions on the kind of respectful language that should be used when discussing strengths and shortcomings.

Within a mutually agreeable time frame, reviews are returned to the cochairs, who check them for appropriate language and tone and then return them to the submitting author. After reviews are completed and delivered to reviewees, a short debriefing protocol is sent to all parties to find out what worked best about the review process and what could still be improved. The process has already been refined several times based on feedback from IC TIG members and peer review participants.

Expectation of Insight. The main incentive for participating in the peer review is the desire to receive valuable professional feedback about one's written communication. After removing identifying information from their reports, reviewees complete a cover sheet to provide the cochairs and reviewers with important contextual information about the program described in their report. This information helps reviewers to focus their comments on what is most useful in the context of that particular evaluation. Reviewers also work from a set of guiding questions for each element of the report. These questions are based principally on concepts in the *AEA Guiding Principles for Evaluators* (2004), which are expected to inform the practice of all professional evaluators, regardless of the substantive areas in which they work. The overall review framework was also influenced by *The Program Evaluation Standards* (Joint Committee on Standards for Educational Evaluation, 1994), which were written for evaluators of educational programs but also offer solid guidance for communication about evaluations in any field.

The TIG reviewer pool is not yet large enough to match reviews and reports by subject and methodology. However, the focus of the review is on clarity and completeness of written communication rather than on more technical evaluation aspects such as design, data collection, and analysis. To date, most reviewers have reported that reviewing their colleagues' work has given them useful insights about their own writing, regardless of whether they were reviewing a report in their own area of substantive expertise. Submitting evaluators have also responded positively to the constructive and respectful critiques they have received from their peers.

Still to Come

We continue to seek ways to make members of our community aware of the opportunity for peer review and encourage their participation. The membership list has been used to alert members to upcoming orientation workshops. When available, a Web site should be an appropriate and accessible repository for posting review guidelines, guiding questions, the report cover sheet, and other documents. For now, the review process is limited to written evaluation reports. This decision was made in order to launch and pilot the peer review process in a timely manner. In the future, however, the scope of the review process may be broadened to include other work products, such as evaluation plans and data collection tools.

Currently in development is a reviewer database, including preferred subject areas, methodological approaches, and past participation as a peer reviewer. As the reviewer pool grows, this database will enable tracking of reviewers who are being over- or underused. The database may also be used to assess the feasibility of matching reviewers and reviewees by subject and methodology, especially if the peer review process is expanded to include evaluation designs and data collection tools.

Over time, as trends in room for improvement become more obvious, this information can be used to develop targeted professional development offerings for members. As the evaluation profession and the community of independent evaluators continues to mature, the peer review process holds promise for improving practice and identifying common professional development needs.

NEW DIRECTIONS FOR EVALUATION • DOI: 10.1002/ev

References

American Evaluation Association. *Guiding Principles for Evaluators.* July 2004. http://www.eval.org/Publications/GuidingPrinciples.asp. Accessed November 5, 2005.

Joint Committee on Standards for Educational Evaluation. *The Program Evaluation Standards: How to Assess Evaluations of Educational Programs.* (2nd ed.) Thousand Oaks, Calif.: Sage, 1994.

SALLY L. BOND *is president of the Program Evaluation Group, based in Pittsboro, North Carolina.*

MARILYN L. RAY *is the executive director of Finger Lakes Law and Social Policy Center in Ithaca, New York.*

NEW DIRECTIONS FOR EVALUATION • DOI: 10.1002/ev

INDEX

Accountability plan, 73

AEA (American Evaluation Association): CFF (client feedback form) origins at, 97–98; CFF on evaluator adherence to principles of, 102*t*; consultant lifecycle implications for, 39; consultant referral service of, 8; ELC presentation by, 89; ENet and ERS merger creating, 5; evaluation support provided by, 30; information gathered and distributed through, 1, 2, 7. *See also* IC TIG (Independent Consulting Topical Interest Group)

AEA Guiding Principles for Evaluators (2004), 111, 112

AEA Guiding Principles for Evaluators (2005), 110

AEA's Multiethnic-Issues Topical Interest Group, 58

American Evaluation Association, 70

American Journal of Evaluation, 6

Architect role, 73

Austin, J. E., 68, 69, 70

Baker, L., 97

Barber, G. J., 2, 41, 49

Bardach, E., 68

Barrington, G. V., 2, 3, 7, 29, 88

Bellman, G. M., 23

Bitner, M., 96

Block, P., 23

Bond, S. L., 3, 109, 113

Bonnet, D. G., 2, 5, 8, 9, 18

Boundary spanners, 74

Brinkerhoff, R., 88

Bruce, R., 30, 32, 33, 34, 35

Business Brokerage Press, 41

California Association of Homes and Services for the Aging, 70

Capacity-building strategy. *See* ELC (evaluation learning circle)

Caracelli, V., 85

CFF (client feedback form): development of, 97–98; function of, 95; lessons learned and future directions for, 106–107; overview of, 98–99; performance assessment using the, 95–96; pilot testing of, 99–106

Child, J., 68, 69

Clegg, J., 3, 79, 84

Client satisfaction, 96–97, 101*t*

Client-consultant relationships: defining partnerships in, 67–68; during evaluation phase, 74–76; evolution of partnerships, 68–76, 69*fig*; initiation of, 68–71; operations of, 72–74

Coe, B. A., 68

Cohen, C., 3, 85

Collaborative consulting survey: on aspects of effective collaborations, 64–65; on collaborating for diversity, 65–66; collaborative challenges reported in, 63–64; description of respondents to, 59*t*; different experience levels and reported collaboration, 61–63; methodology used in, 58; on reasons for collaborating, 60–61; theoretical context of, 58

Coltman, M. M., 41

Communication: governance and, 72; trust as part of open, 70–71

Compatible goals (client-evaluator), 70

Consultant life cycle stages: growth and expansion, 34–35, 37*t*; inception, 32–33, 37*t*; maturity, 35–36, 37*t*; preinception, 32, 37*t*; survival, 33–34, 37*t*

Consultants: AEA's referral service on, 8; career considerations of independent, 23–27; client relations of, 67–76; IC TIG survey (2004) on, 9–20. *See also* Evaluation consultants

"Consultants' Corner" (*Evaluation Practice*), 6

Consulting business (entrepreneurial), 51–56. *See also* Evaluation consulting business

Cope, J. P., 30

Das, T. K., 70, 73

Davidson, J., 89

de Rond, M., 58

Doino-Ingersoll, J. A., 3, 9, 21, 95, 108

Dowell, K., 3, 95, 108

Dressler, D., 88

Dunn, J. A., Jr., 68

Back Issue/Subscription Order Form

Copy or detach and send to:

Jossey-Bass, A Wiley Imprint, 989 Market Street, San Francisco CA 94103-1741
Call or fax toll-free: Phone 888-378-2537 6:30AM–3PM PST; Fax 888-481-2665

Back Issues: Please send me the following issues at $27 each
(Important: please include series initials and issue number, such as EV101.)

_____

_____

_____

$ _____ Total for single issues

$ _____ Shipping charges:

	Surface	Domestic	Canadian
First item		$5.00	$6.00
Each add'l item		$3.00	$1.50

For next-day and second-day delivery rates, call the number listed above.

Subscriptions: Please ___ start ___ renew my subscription to _New Directions for Evaluation_ for the year 2_____ at the following rate:

U.S.	___ Individual $80	___ Institutional $199
Canada	___ Individual $80	___ Institutional $239
All others	___ Individual $104	___ Institutional $273

Online subscriptions are available via Wiley InterScience!

For more information about online subscriptions visit
www.wileyinterscience.com

$_____ Total single issues and subscriptions (Add appropriate sales tax for your state for single issue orders. No sales tax for U.S. subscriptions. Canadian residents, add GST for subscriptions and single issues.)

___ Payment enclosed (U.S. check or money order only)
___ VISA ___ MC ___ AmEx # _____ Exp. date _____

Signature _____ Day Phone _____
___ Bill me (U.S. institutional orders only. Purchase order required.)

Purchase order # _____

Federal Tax ID13559302   **GST 89102 8052**

Name _____

Address _____

_____

Phone _____ E-mail _____

For more information about Jossey-Bass, visit our Web site at www.josseybass.com

NEW DIRECTIONS FOR EVALUATION
IS NOW AVAILABLE ONLINE AT WILEY INTERSCIENCE

What is Wiley InterScience?

Wiley InterScience is the dynamic online content service from John Wiley & Sons delivering the full text of over 300 leading scientific, technical, medical, and professional journals, plus major reference works, the acclaimed Current Protocols laboratory manuals, and even the full text of select Wiley print books online.

What are some special features of Wiley InterScience?

Wiley Interscience Alerts is a service that delivers table of contents via e-mail for any journal available on Wiley InterScience as soon as a new issue is published online.
Early View is Wiley's exclusive service presenting individual articles online as soon as they are ready, even before the release of the compiled print issue. These articles are complete, peer-reviewed, and citable.
CrossRef is the innovative multi-publisher reference linking system enabling readers to move seamlessly from a reference in a journal article to the cited publication, typically located on a different server and published by a different publisher.

How can I access Wiley InterScience?

Visit http://www.interscience.wiley.com.

Guest Users can browse Wiley InterScience for unrestricted access to journal Tables of Contents and Article Abstracts, or use the powerful search engine.
Registered Users are provided with a *Personal Home Page* to store and manage customized alerts, searches, and links to favorite journals and articles. Additionally, Registered Users can view free Online Sample Issues and preview selected material from major reference works.
Licensed Customers are entitled to access full-text journal articles in PDF, with select journals also offering full-text HTML.

How do I become an Authorized User?

Authorized Users are individuals authorized by a paying Customer to have access to the journals in Wiley InterScience. For example, a University that subscribes to Wiley journals is considered to be the Customer.
Faculty, staff and students authorized by the University to have access to those journals in Wiley InterScience are Authorized Users. Users should contact their Library for information on which Wiley journals they have access to in Wiley InterScience.

ASK YOUR INSTITUTION ABOUT WILEY INTERSCIENCE TODAY!

DATE DUE